AF601579

Art, AI and Culture

Michael Betancourt

published by I'm Press'd, Savannah, GA
www.impressd.net

Cover artwork:
instaglitch_68675185_405686730081637_1401474340170901318_n
copyright © 2019 Michael Betancourt
Courtesy Artists Rights Society (ARS)

FIRST EDITION

I must thank Sara Polak for her prompt to consider the cultural impacts of AI, without which this analysis would never have emerged.

---

contents

7
prelude

9
'the social'

23
permanent autonomous zones (PAZ)

49
a 'moralistic ontology'

69
autonomous aesthetics

97
conclusions

103
notes

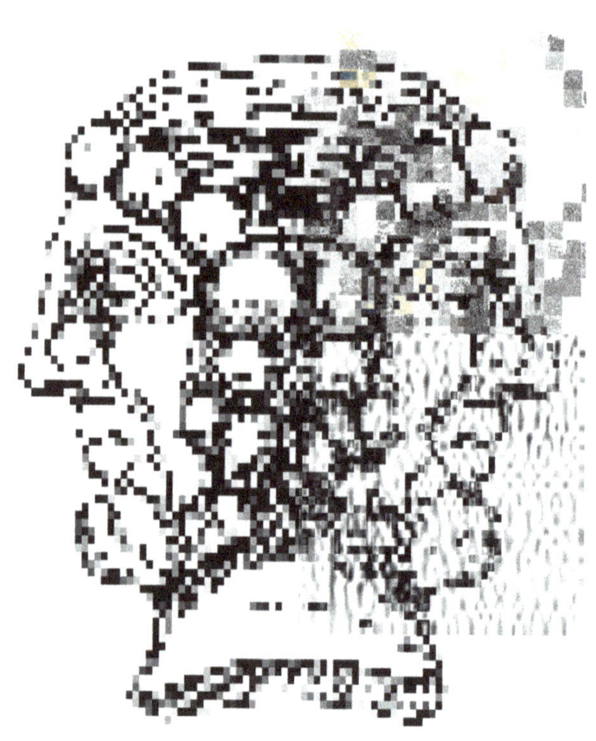

Frontis: *Digital Janus* (2022) by Michael Betancourt, courtesy Artists Rights Society (ARS).

Janus, the Roman god of the beginning and ending of wars should be the patron deity of technology because digital computers, and especially AI, present two faces when confronting human culture: it is simultaneously a ratification of existing beliefs and tendencies, while at the same time it creates opportunities for catastrophic social and cultural change, destroying entire ways of life and replacing them with something that offers the potential for either emancipation or enslavement. These dualities are not easily resolved. The "social identity threats" posed by machine learning activate the lineage of European colonialism and the Enlightenment, a heritage of empires[1] that continues to shape the social, political, and aesthetic affects and applications of automation and autonomous agency (AI) and their significance for human agency (intention). This disruptive technology reveals a framework of cultural values and designations—central to which is the identification of who is allowed to be *human* that converges on the social function of art—that guides its implementations. Contextualizing the law of automation that "whatever can be automated will be" as an ideological demand understands this shift in the conception of capitalism from primarily an economic system to being a system of distribution reflecting social status and privilege as a response to the "social identity threats" posed by extending what were the privileges of the elites to the masses.

The unintelligence of AI and digital automation vanish into the systemic biases this technology instrumentalizes, crystallizing social differences (including class, race, and gender) as mechanisms for maintaining social status and position. These impacts become apparent in how the agency of AI is of an entirely different character than even the determinate, rote *human* judgments it replaces, creating an entirely new type of judgment, the 'technical judgment,' that is mechanically derived with neither concern for, nor capacity to consider the significance of what is being done, revealing the operations of machines are antithetical to the considerations of context and significance that always mediate human judgment.

My analysis proposes a diagnostic theorization of how AI inevitably manifests "social identity threats" through its challenges to the established and familiar system of rights and privileges: the social problems created by autonomous systems can only be resolved through human oversight and social recourse to correct the inevitable harms such automation produces. It is *not* an attempt to describe a hypothetical future, but to acknowledge and then comprehend the axiomatic tendencies of the present. The challenge for any critical analysis of on-going developments is to achieve a contextual understanding with predictive capacity.

Complicating this diagnosis of threats to established order are the specifically legal, fiscal, and cultural disruptions this technology and its operations entangle with its technical operations. The historical lineage of colonialism contained by the aesthetics of both industrialism and Modernism mediates the continuity of AI with the assembly line apparent in the replacement and management of lower status populations by/with automations that suggest a ratification of historical patterns of dominance and repression, rather than emancipation or elevation to higher status through technological innovation.

‘the social’

“We live in capitalism. Its power seems inescapable. But then, so did the divine right of kings.”

—Ursula K. LeGuin, *National Book Awards,* 2014

The fantasy of automation is pernicious. It extrapolates the trajectory introduced by the assembly line, which reduced the role of skilled, intelligent labor in facture by regimenting and fragmenting their tasks, combined with the assumption that human workers are equivalent to the machinery they operate, to conclude they will eventually be completely replaced by it. This unfilled and potentially unfulfillable fantasy illuminates contemporary AI as a *cultural* development whose pseudo-elimination of human labor is a refusal to recognize or consider the actual requirements for human intelligence within the operations of automated systems—a demonstration of the aura of the digital that strips physical requirements and processes from consideration—since AI systems greatly reduce, but do not *entirely* eliminate the need for human oversight or direction in their functioning.[2] This contemporary deskilling of intelligent (immaterial) labor has unknown social consequences since the role of machine learning is limited by the need for human guidance and direction (if not direct, careful oversight and management) to insure appropriate and acceptable outcomes—an intentionality that renders automated labor comparable to the assembly line worker who is responsible for only small parts of a larger task they are neither required nor expected to comprehend.[3] This ideology elevates some forms of human agency and denies others validity, linking the autonomous technical agency of machinery to Enlightenment ideologies that developed a hierarchy for human intellectual labor, emphasizing ‘reflective judgment' as the highest aspect of being-human. These philosophical foundations remain immanent.

Considering the question *'What does AI automate?'* finds its answer in the *agency* that is definitional for capitalism, a social and economic system that reflects the Enlightenment obsession with human agency as the essential constituent for being-human, enshrining it in capitalism as a "commodity exchanged for a wage." The automation of art and creative tasks by AI reveals the distinctions between "reflective" and "determinative" agency are artificial, cultural constructs that are refractions of the prestige associated with the task itself. But the emergence of AI does not alter the social standing attached to tasks—a "sanitation engineer" retains the social standing of a "janitor," and receives a correspondingly low wage, while the 'creative' labor of the CEO is compensated at a much higher rate and has a much higher social status and position: the more essential the labor for brute survival, the lower social its status and position. Recognizing these ideological foundations continue to shape digital capitalism makes the differentials in wages paid to different types of agency/labor coherent: the high wages and social position assigned to the intellectual labor of managerial decisions (reflective judgments) versus that of manual labor (determinative judgments) unite wage differentials and the degree of self-directed agency with class, which then directs attention to *who* performs the labor. These separations in status and role are convergent with *identity—who* is linked to *which* type of agency—the question of wages and employment expresses more than mere economic values as/in social status and position. It demonstrates the heritage of colonialism.

To reconsider the impacts of AI on human agency via a new question, *'Whose labor does AI automate?'* interrogates these linkages between expressions of class, the fantasy of automation, and the collective social organization that defines *culture*—all those ideas that offer a chance at freedom or peace, as well as oppression and violence. They can promote civilization, democracy, and liberation, while simultaneously becoming barriers to change, justice, and emancipation.

AI and digital automation directly affects the moderately skilled workers (a bachelor's degree is typically the entry point into "white color" labor) who are the descendants of the manual labor ("blue collar" labor) replaced by earlier forms of physical automation in previous waves of technological innovation. These workers who are most likely to be impacted by AI are the class within human labor that were *re*skilled following the displacements of earlier factory automation: the people who changed jobs from those requiring manual skill to those whose immaterial tasks define the "information economy."[4] The replacement of this intelligent skilled labor by AI is not simply the automation of "routine," predictable physical and cognitive tasks, but a shift in production that renders the cognitive labor of "white color" workers performing rote tasks as an *identical* commodity to that of any other factory process subject to assembly line fragmentation.

These cultural, political, and economic convergences are 'the social,' but since there are critical theories that argue 'the social' no longer exists under globalization,[5] even posing these questions about societal structure becomes problematic.[6] The present analysis accepts 'the social' as a reification, a simplification, that has a rhetorical utility to identify those dimensions of human relations poised between concerns with individual agency and the constraints imposed by clearly defined and formally organized apparati (such as corporations, governments, or religious organizations)[7] that are an amorphous, but particularly unitary limit on action arising at the interface of governing and governed, not merely as a description of class struggle, but as an affect originating in those aspects of human society which are indicative of the societal hierarchy itself—*culture*.

AI poses a challenge to any analysis of 'the social.' The fantasy of automation is not simply an ideological construct that ignores the physical costs and material demands of production, but a realization that this expression of the social hierarchy and its pseudo-feudal distinctions separating labor from management arises in the degree and extent to which different classes are allowed access to *leisure*: social status is always an act of exclusion that defines *identity*, established by enforcing the boundaries of social distinction and maintaining historical privileges.[8] Understanding AI's cultural impacts on 'the social' begins by recognizing the axiomatic demand to replace all of human labor with machinery (and recover human wages as lost profits) is essential to the valorization of agency created in capitalism's "externalization of productive action," but the illusion of production-without-consumption created by digital automation is merely propositional, and that human agency cannot actually be sold, only *hired*—placed in service of another's desires.[9] Facture necessarily inserts an intermediary between any reflective conception that sets production in motion and the actual production itself, reinforcing its dependence on human agency: AI is rarely *autonomous,* even if machine learning is the apotheosis of this desire to remove the intelligence of human workers entirely from the production process. Machine learning necessitates direct human action to insure its appropriate and reliable operation.

Nevertheless, the cultural changes and social reorganization into a 'society of leisure' that AI suggests by its displacements of human labor (and the claims of the fantasy of automation) demands social expansions of *leisure* that are not a matter of *never,* merely *partial*, and *not yet.* This continual and essential anticipation of what is always already a refusal of the realities of facture and the need for human oversight of machinery is a reflection of the aura of the digital, that same ideology that also justifies granting autonomous processes a freedom from oversight or consideration of their collateral impacts: *what happens to those people whose labor, which has been the foundation for their survival and the justification for their existence, disappears?*— "social identity threats" produced by increasing automation and the use of autonomous systems does not require the mythic 'full automation' where no humans engage in labor for its impacts to be apparent. Even small disruptions in the quantity of human labor required in production are sufficient to undermine and alter 'the social' within the on-demand and just-in-time distribution systems of digital capitalism. As AI expands upon the industrial trend of automating low level tasks, but now addresses tasks that require rote human intelligence, it displaces labor from the types of skilled employment developed to replace the factory work that was automated during the twentieth century.

As the *Brookings Institute* has noted about the deployment of AI, when labor's exposure to being replaced is plotted first against educational attainment, and then across occupations' wage percentiles, the workers most prone to replacement are those in office administration, production, transportation, and food preparation, even though they represent only one-quarter of all jobs whose tasks are potentially automatable. More secure types of labor are united by their non-routine activities or the need for interpersonal intelligence (affective labor), but not by high social status.[10] *Who* automation replaces is unquestionably an issue of class and social dynamics:

> Those with bachelor's degrees will be much more exposed to AI than less-educated groups, and the parallel finding that workers in higher-wage occupations will be much more exposed than lower-wage workers. The exposure curve peaks at the 90th percentile, suggesting that while middle- and upper-middle-class workers are likely to be impacted by artificial intelligence, the most elite workers—such as CEOs—appear to be somewhat protected.[11]

The otherwise mutually exclusive range of tasks that include complex, creative professional and technical labor (such as art) that have high educational requirements and social prestige, along with tasks in low prestige personal care and domestic service are all connected through their subservience to higher classes in the societal hierarchy. The Covid-19 pandemic made these connections between wage labor and social status and position apparent; continuity of work in these low status occupations enabled the majority population to move into isolation to avoid infection in an attempt to mitigate the spread of disease, while the low status labor remained in public despite the risks—ironically revealing that 'essential labor' is performed by a socially disposable population.[12]

Although capitalist automation has consistently replaced those classes of employment that are routine and predictable throughout its history, leaving tasks that require greater flexible intelligence unchanged, a bifurcation of reflective judgment from physical activity masks the digital's parasitic dependence on human agency to initiate, oversee, and manage operations. Technological change defines each stage of this increasingly complex industrialization, from hand labor to machinery, then from mechanization to automation and AI—but each advancement is also a liquidation of specific types of skilled production, first as the automation of material (physical) labor, then as autonomous agency that replaces immaterial (intellectual) labor. This expansion intensifies the shift from manual skills to intellectual expertise, reflecting how this complex machinery employed in production performs both low skill and unskilled tasks automatically, leaving the human operator to perform reflective, intelligent labor.[13]

The labor and cultural reform movements inspired by earlier critiques may have only produced *luxury* items for wealthy factory owners, their ideation has left a significant and lasting cultural mark by redefining aesthetic value to coincide with the evidence of human action. What appears to contemporary thought as an ontological dimension of *identity* (being-human as a distinction from machinery, whether automated or autonomous) is a product of European cultural conflicts prompted by the regimentation of the factory in the nineteenth century that preceded the later regimentation and fragmentation of the assembly line, but anticipates its minimization of human intellectual (immaterial) labor in facture.

The failures of AI/automation become obvious in the emergent role for affective labor as amelioration of its harms by addressing those collateral damages that are the result of inappropriate operations of autonomous systems and their incapacity to quantify social nuances, such as concerns with justice, that have historically modified human action. Unlike the 'essential labor' responsible for facture who have been continuously subject to demands for increased productivity, greater efficiency, and reduced costs, the "white collar" jobs subject to AI replacement have been historically resistant to the fragmentation of the assembly line. The everyday activities of middle management that allocates and directs labor have not been subject to the same pressures of automation prior to the development of AI; that the highest managerial levels are excluded from these developments is a reflection not of their greater complexity, but of individuals in those positions capacity to protect themselves from the challenges of autonomous agency by controlling its development.

Technological replacement produces the issue of surplus labor. Nevertheless, the social impacts of AI are not simply questions of employment or wages, but of which and whose *identity* is regarded as intrinsically significant, and whose is merely a vehicle for valorization. Individual agency and questions of *identity* are entangled with 'the social' and expressed via the degrees of freedom granted to the personal choices and actions which remain (inherently, always) descriptive of its scope, especially during times of cultural change. The prosaic understanding of *identity* as a unique identifier, a label, that differentiates both individuals and groups also informs its role within the database that enables the semiotic valorization of digital capitalism. AI reveals these ambivalently convergent dimensions of *identity* by demonstrating its reification in/as the database; this capture is a crucial aspect of digital capitalism, not as a vehicle for liberation, but as a mechanism for containment, monitoring, and control apparent in the paradox of agency—greater expressions of human agency only result in a greater capture and valorization of the individual, rather than their emancipation.

Although the fantasy of automation appears to offer a future free from oppression and the horrors of industrialism and mindless, regimented labor, it has yet to deliver on that potential. Instead, this ideology reiterates the overly reductive proposition that Buckminster Fuller posed in the middle of the twentieth century—*utopia or oblivion?*—which makes the importance of the cultural impacts of technological change apparent. The 'society of leisure' that struggles to emerge as automation displaces human labor from its central place in the production of value suggests a specifically social challenge that elides *idleness* through a reconception of nonproductive time as a commodity that is recaptured by the valorization of *leisure*-as-consumption.[14] Acts of self-revelation that have proliferated online are the immaterial substance that makes the compartmentalization of individuals possible via data that statistically models their interests, cultural concerns, and political beliefs—all before delivering any bespoke messaging selected by AI. The social affect accentuated by this individualization suggests an increased centering of individual desires and expectations for *personalized* interactions at all times—an infantile onanism of the self where AI provides a continuous palliative reinforcement-response. The psychological regression this affect suggests is foreshadowed in the disinhibitions already apparent in online communications and interactions (such as "trolling") where antisocial and narcissistic behaviors are commonplace.

Monitoring these acts of human agency is the primary source of value in digital capitalism (*data*), even as their rote implementation is the physical source of valorization and profit generation. This ideological codependency in capitalist relations is what the fantasy of automation assuages by dismissing the recognition of human labor in the management and operation of AI systems, reducing the cognitive dissonance this ideology produces. These economics reify distinctions in class position that all social strata are invested in maintaining, even those in a subservient position: wages are proxies for social status and position, and in capitalist economies such as the United States they create social and political mechanisms convergent with *identity* and educational attainment. Digital surveillance is central to this attempt to quantify 'the social' as an immaterial commodity (*data*) by entrenching and expanding valorization as a semiotic production without restriction or restraint. The agnotology::surveillance dynamic maintains this status quo through a process of affect and individuation (itself an expression of concerns with *identity*) where economic developments are also cultural expressions: the undefined and open nature of the art world[15] corresponds precisely to this all-encompassing framework valorizing 'the social.' Aesthetic production illuminates these dynamics because it is the explicit demonstration of social status and position.

AI's dehumanizing of intelligent labor (immaterial production) renders the distinct phases of ideation, design, and fabrication as a new pair of valorizations: the human (*utility*) and the semiotic (*value*) that both depend on the operations of AI and its manipulations of the database whose 'open' acceptance treats every *identity* as equivalent and proceeds without concern for the significance of that individual. This egalitarian flattening prompts rejections and resistance as it conflicts with received tradition: one needs only to consider the "wage gap" that pays males and females different wages for the same labor to recognize that *identity* cannot be separated from the social functions of agency, a factor that also makes the consideration /art/ of interest to considerations of AI when confronting differentials in social status and position.

Societal hierarchies mark all aspects of 'the social' (including the obvious dimensions of class, race, ability, and gender, as well as occupation, educational attainment, and generational wealth) via aesthetics—expressions of *leisure* and *luxury* that entangle the social status connected to human agency with *identity*.

AI disrupts established hierarchies, creating powerful "social identity threats" from how digital capitalism reifies the metaphysics of 'the social' as instrumentalities for production and social capture in an expansive physical and intellectual marketplace, globalized and cosmopolitan, that accepts and accommodates any challenge, neutralizing even the most confrontational ideas as sites for valorization and economic exploitation. It is a process that depends on the containment of political protest and critique in a domain entirely separate from political action; however, that separation is challenged by how AI transforms human agency and expands *leisure* and *luxury* to undermine their social function as demonstrations of class, position, and hierarchy. The expansive nature of the database to enable, document, and valorize any and all behaviors directly conflicts with historical traditions and dogmas (such as those enforced through religious edict) and enters into explicit conflict with the historical organization of 'the social.' Considerations of *identity* provide a lens through which these conflicts come into focus as instances of the paradox of agency which renders all choices made by human agency equivalent via their storage as data. "Culture war" is an inevitable product of this colonization of social relationships.

The most obvious application of this automated production is one where AI is almost fully hidden: the horizontal capacity to communicate through the algorithmic matching of message with audience. This force magnifier allows the circulation and amplification of belief via a bespoke targeting of messages to specific individuals for any purpose (financial, political, propagandistic). This mobilization becomes evident through the use of social media as a 'viral' communications system. Digital technology does not alter the twentieth century's concerns with 'mass communication,' offering instead the logical expansion of that messaging through the sorting and delivery capacities of AI: a more precise, targeted message tuned to meet the desires of their receiving audience.[16] Reaching an 'audience of one' depends on flexibility and automation, coupled with the valorization of *identity.* This subtle form of social capture is an illusory freedom of participation and democracy.

Industrialization lays the foundations[17] for this use of machine learning because AI is the central mechanism of all those operations that redefine traditional conceptions of *identity* as new opportunities for accumulation, in the process upending the commandment to "become oneself" common to the heritage of human agency as self-definition. The processes and procedures of the database fuse the social functions of *identity* with its role in surveillance to valorize 'the social': the human subject is always, already, and exclusively conceived in terms of their behaviors as all being types of productive action, which digital capitalism then captures as a catalyst for *value* production (via surveillance).

The disruptions created by autonomous agency converge with and continue those historical lineages of class and position that AI instrumentalizes as the parameters and role of *identity.* The valorization process neutralizes some threats via agnotology while creating another: the expansion of *leisure.* This abstracted, impersonal, and structural signifier of distinction is divorced from the individuals it identifies, mirroring the historical abstraction of 'uniform labor' in economic analyses of industrial capitalism.

'The social' is not a mass of individuals guided by the principles of rational self-interest, but a morass of competing and contradictory tendencies that have become granular, monitored, manifold through the data gathered by pervasive monitoring—an atomistic awareness of the interface between aggregate behaviors and personal desires that has transformed the historical conception of the "mass audience" into a precisely targeted collective body—*out of many, one*—not mere affects accompanying a fixed caste system or predetermined set of interactions, but a fluid and constantly shifting morass of enculturation being valorized and transformed into *potential value* by the operations of the database via *identity*.

The digital holds social status and privilege in suspension between individual or group rights, and the fluidly contingent relations of human agency. Accommodating this shift decenters labor from being the foundation for all the financial and economic structures of capitalism. The mechanisms for this predatory paradigm establish a self-fulfilling model for valorization that is reinforced by the affective role of "social identity threats": racism, sexism, homophobia, and religious beliefs combine with misinformation and agnotology to neutralize opposition to digital capitalism's colonization of 'the social.' *Identity* assists and rationalizes the irrationality of agnotology by reinforcing divisions that derive from a new type of alienation—one produced by having all choices rendered equivalent, leaving the human agency in their selection meaningless.

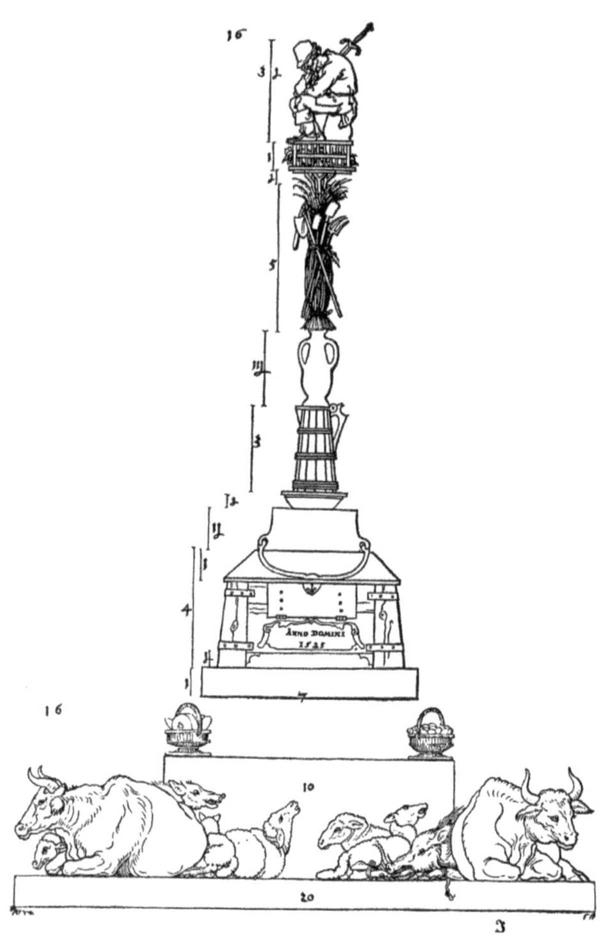

Figure 1: "Monument to the Vanquished Peasants" published in *Unterweisung der Messung* [*Treatise on Measurement*] (1525) by Albrecht Dürer. Woodcut print illustrating his commentary on a monument commemorating a victory over the peasant army in the 1525 German Peasant's War.

The specific difficulty with assessing the impacts of AI on 'the social' emerges from confusion of worries about technological unemployment that are as old as the industrial revolution[18] with anxieties about technological change threatening the established stability of the existing societal hierarchy.[19] Contemporary fears about AI and fantasies of a 'robot rebellion'[20] are echoes of historical fears about serf rebellions against the feudal system that metamorphosed into concerns about slave rebellions and colonial uprisings against early capitalism [Figure 1].[21] These transpositions obscure the complexity of the cultural situation emergent with AI under digital capitalism. Expansions of elite privileges to new social classes threatens the existing hierarchy by undermining the perception of privilege and exception created by the systematic devaluation of "others"—those specific castes of individuals who are placed outside the "human." This status is at the heart of issues surrounding questions of *identity. Who* is allowed the status being-human is a cultural perception that is historically problematic for the Enlightenment project. "Human rights" assumes a specific valence when confronting this heritage and its contemporary lineage under digital capitalism—they have an apparently contradictory status where not everyone receives them. As a privilege enshrined by law in the *United States Constitution*, (Article 1, Section 2, Clause 3), this Enlightenment proposition about *identity* is explicit:

> Representatives and direct Taxes shall be apportioned among the several States which may be included within this Union, according to their respective Numbers, which shall be

> determined by adding to the whole Number of free Persons, including those bound to Service for a Term of Years, and excluding Indians not taxed, three fifths of all other Persons.

Written in 1787, this document is a model of Enlightenment concerns with agency expressed via democratic freedom, yet the "Three–Fifths Compromise" provides a legal basis for the limited status being-human for the enslaved and their descendants: they only count for three-fifths of a regular citizen, and women are not counted at all. These racist and sexist foundations are (unfortunately) integral to the Enlightenment's democratic tradition; this section was only rescinded in 1868, three years *after* the United States' civil war ended. However, the extension of status the fourteenth amendment created in 1868 did not include women—they only gain full legal rights in the United States in 1919.[22] The colonial heritage of this racism and sexism instrumentalizes issues of *identity*, matching them with an ideology that restricts "human" to only certain parts of society, which is then articulated by law. The expansion of privileges (and the status of being-human) is a "social identity threat" that coincides with the rise of capitalism and the simultaneous expansion of *leisure* to ever larger sections of society. The rise of democracy and its opposition to autocracies of all types reinforces these economic and social developments towards greater freedom and justice. For AI to reproduce these historical biases is likely inevitable and should not be a surprise to anyone—they are deeply embedded in 'the social,' haunting both *de jure* and *de facto* systems of privilege based on *identity*.

Acknowledging that being-human is *not* a 'status' dependent on *agency*, but an ontological state requiring specific recognitions of natural rights has required a cultural (and legal) shift that demands societies abandon the historical stratification of 'the social.' Digital capitalism's expansive pressures for access to new markets and increased valorization to generate profit creates a cultural force conflicting with the inherited selectivity of who is allowed to claim the status of being-human that is the converse of nineteenth century art historian John Ruskin's observations in *The Stones of Venice* (1853) about labor as "animated tools" which only become human by being granted self-agency—i.e. without agency they are *not* human:

> Understand this clearly: you can teach a man to draw a straight line, and to cut one; to strike a curved line, and to carve it; and to copy and carve any number of given lines or forms, with admirable speed and perfect precision; and you find his work perfect of its kind: but if you ask him to think about any of those forms, to consider if he cannot find any better in his own head, he stops; his execution becomes hesitating; he thinks, and ten to one he thinks wrong; ten to one he makes a mistake in the first touch he gives to his work as a thinking being. But you have made a man of him for all that. He was only a machine before, an animated tool.[23]

These social and cultural differentials inform Ruskin's appraisal of productive labor. Refusing the intellectual capacities of the mass labor employed in the factories not only dehumanizes that human labor as living machinery, it also justifies its dehumanization. His embrace of the 'authorial hand' as a counter to the anonymous machine becomes a demand for an aesthetics of 'authenticity' through the identification of 'hand-made' with *luxury* production in the Arts and Crafts workshops created by William Morris.[24] The 'human touch' provided a mechanism for distinguishing "art" from the slick, polished uniformity of industrial processes (both the "kitsch" manufactured by factories, and the highly detailed photographs that replaced portraiture in art), where this shift to displays of being 'hand-made' makes the 'intentional function' evident through its emphasis on those material markers that denote the human "hand," or that appear to challenge the autonomous operations of the digital machine (such as the contemporary genre of Glitch Art[25] where digital errors become expressive aesthetic gestures). This direct symptom of the Romantic desire to negate the industrial revolution[26] associates *luxury* with the *exclusivity* created by the high costs of the traditional processes and methods used by Morris and his Arts and Crafts workshop.[27] The lineage of this tradition continues to inform the *exclusivity* of *luxury* (art) through the uniqueness and authenticity of the personal experience, conceived and produced in opposition to the mass reproduction of media.[28]

An elevation in social status to being-human does not follow from changes in labor, even if economic demands support its expansion, but from empathy and recognition that the status "human" is a birthright, rather than a privilege. However, *who is accepted* as "human" and *who is not* informs the Enlightenment belief in the importance of self-directed agency, and a colonial heritage whose rejections of racial, social, sexual, and cultural difference have shaped all aspects of European culture, both in the subcontinent and especially in its former colonies, including the United States. The dehumanization produced by the alienation of labor from their agency is also a refusal of their humanity that echoes the cultural and political alienation of the colonized; it is useful to remember that native populations in the colonies were viewed as potential slaves and as disposable labor in service to European empire: William Blake created an imperial depiction of racial difference [Figure 2]

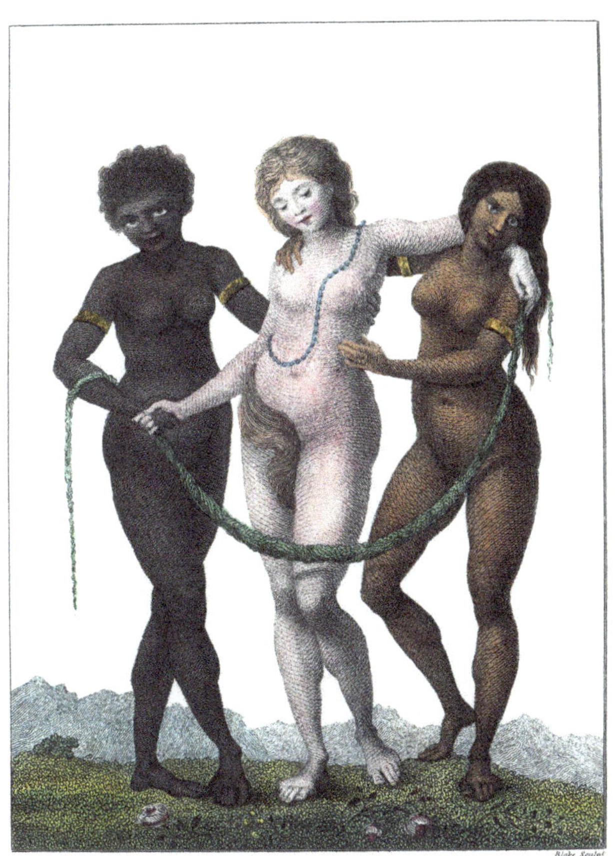

Figure 2: *Europe supported by Africa & America* (December 1, 1792) by William Blake, printed for J. Johnson, St. Paul's Church Yard, and J. Edwards, Pall Mall, England, 1796.

where Europe is the pure (white) woman who takes support from her hand-maidens (whose golden armbands mark them as both foreign and servile), a composition that visually places non-Europeans in a secondary role. The later photograph by Josep-Maria Cañellas [Figure 3] presents live models as allegorical figures: Europa in the classical pose of a Venus, attended by her servant, Africa. Almost a century apart, these depictions communicate the same colonial message of dominance and servitude.

European encounters with non-European cultural traditions reveal colonialism is not merely a response to their discoveries of foreign societies, but also demonstrates how non-European cultures and religions become vehicles for European fantasies about their own status.[29] A doubly patronizing imprint of cultural appropriation and the racist supposition that these foreign traditions were "primitive," informs nineteenth and twentieth century social, cultural, and aesthetic concerns with *purity*. This ideation connects Romanticism's anguish over the lost spirituality they believe was destroyed by industrialism to Modernity. The dehumanizing claims that the indigenous populations of the Americas, Australia, and Africa are examples of a 'noble savage'—a status between distinction and discrimination—are common nineteenth century expressions of this ideology that found a direct and literal presentation in the 'human zoos' common to the World's Fairs of the 1800s and 1900s.[30]

The relationship of Romantic challenges to industrialization and the implementation of contemporary AI is obvious: new mechanical processes which increase worker productivity also replace (or displace) the *human*, substituting machinery for labor. For Ruskin and Romanticism, when the laborer decides what to do, they become *human,* versus their role in the factory where they

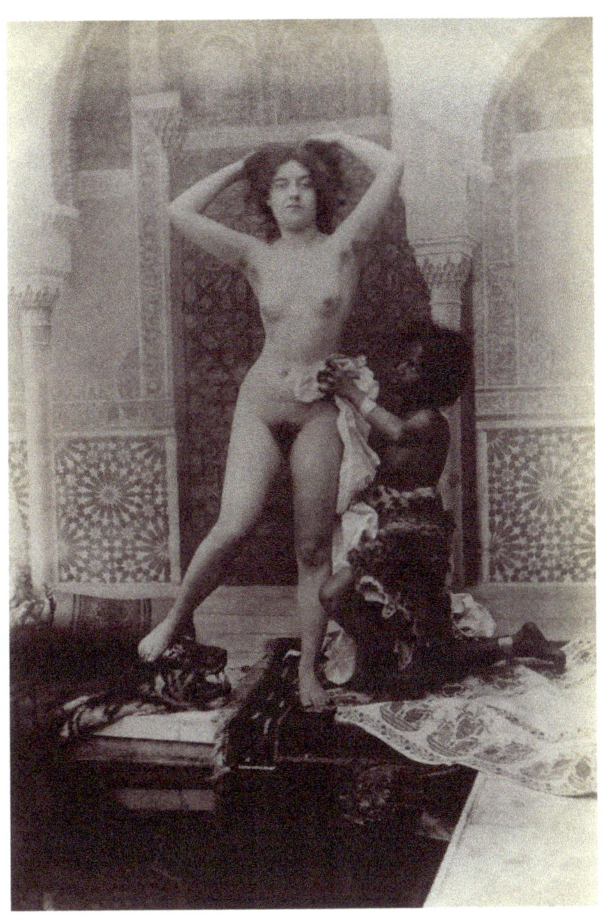

Figure 3: *Europa Attended by Africa* (1890) sepia toned albumin photograph made in Paris by Spanish photographer Josep-Maria Cañellas.

do not make these decisions, acting instead as "animated tools." A similar proposition about labor as a complementary dimension of mechanization appears in Karl Marx's "fragment on machinery":

> But, once adopted into the production process of capital, the means of labor passes through different metamorphoses, whose culmination is the *machine,* or rather, an *automatic system of machinery* (system of machinery: the *automatic* one is merely its most complete, most adequate form, and alone transforms machinery into a system), set in motion by an automaton, a moving power that moves itself; this automaton consisting of numerous mechanical and intellectual organs, so that the workers themselves are cast merely as its conscious linkages.[31]

Marx is not describing a cybernetic organism, but rather the subsumption of human labor within a fully regimented process over which they have no agency. The limited degrees of freedom accorded to the human workers in the factory displaces their agency through the concept of *prima causa*: they are not the ones who choose to perform their labor as they do; their agency is in the service of another's will. Control over bodily autonomy (especially for women) reveals this ideology precisely because the operations of social authority have always concerned what is done to and with human (and female) bodies. Human labor functions in tandem to the machinery they operate, and both serve the desires of their masters. The capitalist hiring of agency for a wage disenfranchises labor from acts of self-directed agency—reserving the status 'human' for the managerial elites. The contemporary replacement of "management" positions by AI is a betrayal of the industrial social contract where the advancement from rote physical labor into office labor would be accompanied by a rise in social standing.

The skill and knowledge of this human "animated tool" are insignificant for understanding capitalist production—allowing the conception of one human laborer as interchangeable with any other (including their replacement by AI)—since the only agency that matters is the one deciding the rules. The managerial decisions rendered by labor via production displace individual choice, linking industrialization to the distinctions separating art (the design of the commodity) from craft (its facture), and the definition of capitalism itself. Ruskin's *aesthetic* emphasis on the delay and pause that labor takes to "consider if he cannot find any better in his own head" identifies the immaterial action of managerial (reflective) agency as a separate process from implementing those decisions. This ideology emphasizes self-directed agency, conceiving factory production as a dehumanizing reflection of class position; his description of emancipating labor from the industrial factory involves the same assumptions that inform the "Luddite fallacy"[32]—fear that labor displaced which does not find a new function in human society has lost its right to exist. This Romanticism reveals itself in the proposition of the "*ghost in the machine*" as a simultaneous expression of philosopher Rene Descartes' mind/body dualism that splits the physical from the mental, and a counter-proposition to the industrial metaphor active in behaviorist psychology, a transcendent attempt to separate intellectual capacity (mind) from its physicality (body) conceived in opposition to the mechanical terms adopted by the physical sciences as they displaced traditional religious beliefs.[33] However, whether labor is done by humans or machines is irrelevant to this construction of social status since the societal hierarchy is relativistic: 'the social' is a function of immanent context and encounter rather than an *a priori* given.

The capitalist construction of *identity* links the disparate concerns of aesthetics, social status, and position with the differential valuations of agency through the ideology of 'autonomous achievement' in nineteenth century industrialism: disciplined pursuit of self-interest was a "moral good" justifying and justified by extreme imbalances in wealth and prosperity, understanding them as paradoxically *promoting* the general welfare of the whole society.[34] Wealth was a proxy for those things establishing an individual's position within the social hierarchy, and justifying the entire social order as a demonstration of personal morality.

The judgments AI enables for their human audiences function relationally,[35] as comparisons between the immanent encounter and an internalized, idealized model that makes the role of transcendence in human interpretive process explicit via the cues of position and importance that determine individual consciousness, beliefs, actions; forcing an acknowledgment that the collective operations of AI systems as arbiters of access, distribution, and production will inevitably conflict with *identity* as a distinct expression of individuation, both by selection and apprehension. The entanglement of social status and position with expressions of *leisure* and *luxury* is a Gordian knot of mutually reinforcing and differentiating choices that renders production of 'the self' an instrumentalized and reified *cogito* that for contemporary *identity* is linked to demands for uniqueness and difference that paradoxically derive from collective identifications: group memberships based in class, ethnicity, religion, etc. and which facilitate pervasive monitoring and consumer prediction. These 'unique identifiers' enable the valorization made possible by the amorphous, absorptive complex of agnotology::surveillance. The obsession with prediction and control that defines this apparatus is a product of its self-reinforcing operations that demand continual expansion, shared by digital capitalism's attempts to render the state of information as an immanent instrumentality.[36]

Anticipatory forecasts of human action are a common part of the use of AI in marketing and demographics as mechanisms to track, trace, and locate individuals (despite efforts at anonymization). It defines the emergent practice of "behavioral stylometry."[37] This role for *identity* is symptomatic of how every existing society has always used available technologies as a mechanism of control. The attempt to transfer the commercial application of demographics where computer analytics predict consumption trends to other areas of human society demonstrates the expansive nature of this technology and its tendency to disenfranchise human agency through a process of containment where only a limited set of options are made available. This conception of the digital as a system of autonomous administration (a role it already performs as digital rights management and through the security apparatus) allows its operations to be reified by AI to catch "precrimes"—potential criminal acts—in advance of their being committed by monitoring and preemptively policing those populations placed at the margins of 'the social.' This conjunction of AI, human relations, demographics, and pervasive monitoring reifies the societal hierarchy as instrumentality.

This use of AI for moralizing surveillance is explicit in the 'Technology Platform for Social Intervention' (*TPSI*) created by Microsoft and deployed in Argentina that demonstrates the differential between *identity* as an expression of freedom and self-actualization, and its function in AI systems as a mechanism for dominance and control. This system uses AI to attempt to prognosticate who, "five or six years in advance, with first name, last name, and address, which girl—future teenager—is 86 percent predestined to have an adolescent pregnancy."[38] The program's emphasis in both data collection and monitoring was on low income populations, precisely those people whose social class is used by higher class groups to define them as criminal, profligate, untrustworthy because of their poverty, ethnicity, and national origin. The racist overtones of this program should not be ignored, but neither are they unexpected. The claim by *TPSI* that a certain *identity* is "86 percent predestined to have an adolescent pregnancy" is an attempt to identify and then administratively contain adolescent pre-pregnancy; the *TPSI* criminalises social behaviors that are not in themselves criminal. Attempts to justify these systems as vehicles for increased freedom is a rhetorical sleight-of-hand that depends on their *a priori* containment disappearing from consideration following the aura of the digital's elision of physicality.

Restrictive control is immanent in the training data used to create AI systems, a factor that also tends to render their bias invisible to the system's designers in a reflection of the assumptions that guide the training process itself. However, the application of these technologies to predict human agency for social relationships in an individualized fashion renders this population's autonomy insignificant, an action which is both paternalistic (in that they are no longer granted their own agency) and historically derived (these are the populations used as manual labor in factories and fields). The predictive regulation of their activities follows from the behaviorist claim that human intention operates in a mechanical fashion—it transforms the low status population into living machinery, subject to the same predictive and operational constraint and control as any other mechanism. *TPSI* demonstrates the continued impacts of restrictions on being-human within the societal hierarchy. The convergence of historical and contemporary repression and management of low status populations suggests the role of bias in AI is an instrumentalization of established patterns of dominance and repression, rather than a force that emancipates or elevates low status populations to higher status through technological innovation.

The specific powerlessness created by *TPSI* unquestionably instrumentalizes the historical control systems of industrialization. Its restrictive 'degrees of freedom' reify the limited potentials chosen by the system's designers. Restrictions on the agency of labor in the past becomes a justification to monitor and restrain their descendant's agency in the present and future: the constraints it creates are self-fulfilling prophesies. The demographically and geographically defined population addressed by this study aligns with historical populations seen as problematic and requiring administration by those in authority. All those peoples whose social status and position in society, and role in industrial facture as the disposable and marginalized labor—reflections of racism, classism and sexism—demonstrate the imbalances and excesses that are instrumentalized through autonomous technology.

At the heart of *TPSI* is a concern with temporal regimentation that is a perennial feature of human society, whether in the cyclic migrations of herders, or the seasonal sowing and tending of crops, or even the metered labor of the industrial factory. Measurements of time are inscribed at the foundation of the technical enterprise itself; the marking and arrangement of time is not open to question, nor to alternatives. Performances of *identity* and *leisure* thus become signifiers of social status—a reciprocal and self-reinforcing system where "human" is a class privilege reiterated by the cultural distinction between *idleness* and *leisure*: twin values that identify the same activity—*time expended in ways that are not productive*. To *not work* is an historical privilege enjoyed by the elites as an expression of the 'society of leisure.' Consequently, time management is a concern not only of economic production, but of social order and the maintenance of the status quo.

The heritage of empire is unavoidable: *Greenwich Mean Time* (*GMT*) provides the initial reference for every time zone in the world since it is where longitude begins—degree zero at the "Prime Meridian" located at the Greenwich Observatory in London, England. Unlike latitude which is fixed by the Earth's rotation, this arbitrary origin point inscribes European imperialism (and the British Empire) on a global scale, ordering geographic space around an imperial island and casting the rest of the world at increasing distance from that *locus vivendi*. The imperial center is inherently managerial, while the colony performs the productive labor (or produces the materials that are converted into industrial commodities elsewhere).

Time becomes instrumental through the mundane technology of digital navigation, itself dependent on a satellite-based global positioning system that employs a network of radio signals to define position precisely in an expression of a fundamentally colonial metric; the AI system that drives a vehicle does not merely look at the landscape, it consults these invisible systems of location and temporality to navigate that physical space, knowing its way through the environment because these earlier cultural decisions are the formative basis of later technological application. The instrumentalization of measurement enshrines demands for physical infrastructure: a stable power grid, well maintained roads and bridges, and unimpeded access to the internet to manage its logistics are central to globalization, as the People's Republic of China's "Personal Information Protection Law" demonstrates by showing the incompatibility between privacy and digital capitalism's need for the unimpeded movement of data through the internet. When this law came into effect on November 1, 2021 ships entering or inside Chinese territorial waters disappeared from the international *Automatic Identification System* used to track and identify maritime traffic; the movement of this information is essential to the system of globalized production.[39] The embedding of these cultural formulations of colonialism within/as the digital system establishes them as autonomous frameworks, resistant to human demands, that allow determinate operations to proceed without the need for human oversight. It inscribes historical imperialism and capitalism's differential valuations of human agency into 'the social,' literally expressed by circulations of commodities and the organization of supply chains, production, and labor emergent as structural relations describing "first world economies" and the "developing economies" that were their colonial (occupied) territories.

Fragmentation such as this Chinese law arise from conflicts over the maintenance of privileges for historically elite groups versus capitalist circuits of *value*. This instability is immanent in digital capitalism's transition from the 'valorization of agency' to the 'valorization of identity' via the automation of pervasive monitoring. This destabilization of the societal hierarchy reveals itself in the contemporary redefinition of "cultural activity" whose democratizing extension of the 'society of leisure' to those groups conceived as resources to consume in production necessitates a redefinition of art and culture. What is apparent in the 2017 *Culture Track* study by the marketing firm LaPlaca Cohen is the radical transformation of *culture* that happened in the first decades of the twenty-first century:

> The narrow niche of culture had expanded to include public parks alongside art museums, food and drink experiences alongside dramatic theater, and street art alongside classical dance. For today's audiences, the definition of culture has democratized even further, possibly to the point of extinction. Activities that have traditionally been considered culture and those that haven't are now on a level playing field, with audiences torn about whether the label "culture" is even applicable. For instance, more than a third of art museum goers did not think art museums were a cultural experience, and over half of theater goers felt the same. In fact, audiences were more likely to consider a street fair or food and drink experience culture than an opera or ballet. This presents a complete paradigm shift. Audiences in 2017 do not place priority or meaning in whether an activity is "culture" or not: it can be anything from Caravaggio to Coachella, Tannhäuser to taco trucks.[40]

The expansion and changed conception of "culture" this study demonstrates is a reflection of those social factors expressive of *luxury* that combine with the expansive valorization of *identity* to articulate "arts and culture" as specifically *performative*. Understanding art as an interactive, social activity was initially advanced by the Relational Artists of the 1990s, such as Rirkrit Tiravanija, who situated their art in the mediation of social relations and behaviors—a positioning that necessarily converted these relationships into commodities.[41] Their exclusivity expresses cultural significance (art) that becomes a marker of social status and position, reaffirming the role of culture as a distinction between different classes. Shifts in the comprehension of art to directly and specifically valorize its role as a 'social activity' inform these transformations. The *Culture Track* report documents the conjunction of a performative and relational *identity* with what had traditionally been the domain of aesthetic objects.

Cultural ideology has become a site for the valorization of social functions shown by *identity,* but these developments were nascent in the 1930s social programs of the United State's Works Progress Administration. Holger Cahill, Director of the WPA, and curator of several exhibitions of American Folk Art at the Museum of Modern Art in New York, comments in his book *Art for the Millions* on the audience for art emerging in the 1930s with the expansions of *leisure* made possible by unionization, decades before the contemporary crisis:

> I do not think that we have weighed sufficiently the meaning of the change from a handicraft to a machine method of production, probably the most revolutionary change in the history of human society. Its effect upon the arts has been catastrophic. It has divorced the artist from the usual vocations of the community and has practically shut off the average man from the arts.[42]

Cahill describes the Romantic desire to integrate art with other aspects of everyday life—an outcome the various Arts and Crafts reformers of the nineteenth century desired—but this development complicates the role of *leisure* as a marker of distinction. Ultimately increasing the audiences who consume the products of the factories provided an economic benefit to expansions of *leisure*, thereby increasing profits and delaying the periodic economic crashes caused by production exceeding the demands and capacity of consumption. The contemporary refusal of historical hierarchies surrounding museums as cultural gatekeepers, expressed by the *Culture Track* report's observation that "art museum goers did not think art museums were a cultural experience," describes the fusion of art and life this lineage sought. However, granting the privilege of *leisure* to larger sections of society has always been countered by the encouragement of labor to link their personal *identity* to their employment.

The contemporary embrace of *identity* as a signifier for freedom and individualism separates contemporary concerns with *identity* from earlier social desires for self-actualization and agency common to nineteenth century concerns with being-human. The role of AI in these societal changes as both driver and descriptor is evident in its refractive and discursive functions as data collector, sorting mechanism, and distribution system that manifests not only relationships of dominance and subservience, but also enables the unsettling of employment and the conversion of *identity* into a form of valorization via surveillance.

Although this transformation of human social behaviors (friendship, politics, shopping, etc.) into a commodity via pervasive monitoring is an expansion of valorization processes, it is not a replacement for past forms of productive action; surveillance is an expansive transformation of 'the social' that has rendered formerly non-economic behaviors into a new form of *unpaid* productive activity (data) that constitutes a parallel realm to the valorization of traditional labor and commodity facture. AI intensifies the new alienation and "social identity threat" that resides not in a loss of agency, but in the *insignificance* of that agency. These dynamically rigid systems reinforce and reinvigorate earlier class privileges and distinctions through their conversion into autonomous systems that mystify the political decisions about who is important and who is not.

Utopian "start-up society" projects are literal attempts to use automation to render the societal hierarchy as fixed system of privileges and rights. Their implementation depends on a combination of governments seceding their authority to a private corporation, and the imposition of controls made possible by digital systems. Digital automation and the instrumentalized metaphor of the "social contract" as actual law are central to these proposals. The city-state *Próspera* (*Prosperous*) is typical: a semi-autonomous, privately run city on the Caribbean island of Roatán in Honduras that was designated a *ZEDE* in 2017, a "zonas de empleo y desarrollo económico" (zone for employment and economic development). This legal status allows it to self-govern independent of the majority of its host nation's laws. It is an example of attempts to establish 'permanent autonomous zones' (*PAZ*) outside legal oversight that parasitically returns the host country to the servile status of a colonial possession.

Próspera reifies *identity* as economic status determines individual rights in an expression of class and social difference that affirms how the agency of labor is not simply ignored, but discounted entirely—except when directed into capitalist valorization.[43] Its hierarchical system is a series of social controls and restrictions, rendering the proxy of wealth as an instrumentalization of social class:

> Residents elect only five of the council's nine members. Landowners vote for two

of the five, with voting power pegged to acreage. Buy more land, buy more votes. *Próspera's* founders choose the four remaining council members, and a six-member super majority is needed to alter policy.[44]

This city-state replaces most legal functions of government with software applications and automation that implements a framework designed to enable the founders to maintain control over their city-state indefinitely because its charter is only superficially democratic. The requirement of a super majority to revise the charter means that no changes can happen unless they are approved by the founders; it gives them veto power over any democratic demands made by the majority of their citizens—a status typically reserved for monarchs. This defensive protection of existing status and privileges is a structural feature of the *PAZ* that enshrines status quo authority as a permanent constraint on the legal organization of this city-state—an expansion of the nineteenth century dogma that economic wealth is the same as moral superiority known as the "Protestant Work Ethic" in the United States.

Digital automation and AI in *Próspera* maintain elite entitlements by transforming fundamental human rights into contingent functions of personal wealth, reflected clearly in the voting system. These expressions of systemic biases derived from historically determined social, political, and economic injustices reveal protections for "social identity" are a structural barrier not only to the fair or just organization of society, but to any type of automation derived from that existing system. AI enables the creation of an autonomously privileged elite whose position is maintained through the technical apparatus and the legal protections attached to its implementation.

A *PAZ* is independent of the state structure in which it is embedded. Unlike its anarchist roots, the "start-up society" model for the *PAZ* employed by projects such as *Próspera* acts to reify existing societal hierarchies by placing them beyond simple legal redress: 'autonomy' is a vehicle for institutionalized bias. The historically colonial relationship replicated (or resurrected) in *Próspera* is a symptom of the globalization which leaves the societies of emerging economies (such as Honduras) in a precarious position in relation to deployment of AI. The *PAZ* reasserts colonial relations as the costs imposed to create opportunities for investment and economic opportunity, expanding them to include wealthy individuals, corporations, as well as the developed nations interacting with these 'developing economies.'

Attempts to implement the fantasy of automation exacerbate the conflicts and fragmentation produced by what are already highly restrictive systems whose operations invoke the aura of the digital in a minimization (or elimination) of human accountability. The automation of social order created by translating historical relations into AI via machine learning merely acts to render these hierarchies resistant to change because AI can only follow the established precedents it has been trained to reproduce, even if it incidentally also instrumentalizes racism, sexism, homophobia and other forms of bias. Coupled with the automation of social status and position, (whether directly via a technology of "social credit," or indirectly by replacing informal social relationships with formal systems of organization), AI makes contemporary attempts to render the existing societal hierarchy resistent to challenge possible. The *PAZ* attempts to maintain the historical privileges accorded to an elite few, against not only the emergent democratizing tendencies expanding *leisure* to formerly indentured classes of labor, but to prevent their "social identity threat." The assumption implicit in the implementation of AI systems in projects such as *Próspera* is that they will ratify elites as a permanent dominant class. AI counters existing, newly emergent, and potential "social identity threats" by transforming what they challenge into a technical dimension of social order, autonomously implemented and maintained. This conjunction marks the function of *identity* as a vehicle for the social regulation of all activity that uses computer technology for a perverse expansion or extension of the contractual relationships and formal administrative functions of digital rights management.

However, the desire to replicate human social relationships via autonomously administered privileges also assumes that the human societies being replaced are static, fixed constellations of importance and unimportance, rather than fluid and unstable collections of tendencies and activities. It is an attempt to rationalize human social organization in the same ways that the assembly line made production more efficient.[45] The problems for this conception of 'the social' are self-evident. Continuous pervasive monitoring is required to instrumentalize relationships that are not a fixed, *a priori* framework, but a dynamic and shifting series of contingent decisions: attempts to render the societal hierarchy as a fixed set of roles and permissions via digital automation of various types (including AI) arise precisely because 'the social' needs constant reinforcement to maintain order—and that order can be rendered moot—any individual's place in a *democratic* hierarchy is always open to change. *PAZ* offers a digital caste system that replaces the historical order of capitalism with a pseudo-feudal system that renders social standing in the post-labor economy as a series of privileges rather than rights. It attempts to instrumentalize the status provided by accumulated wealth: *Próspera* is an attempt to automate the maintenance of class differences, to redefine current positions within the societal hierarchy as perpetual and immobile positions within society.

The shift to administration by AI crystallizes the social system. Harms produced by the fantasy of automation are not necessarily matters for mitigation within such a regime, but are rather symptom-effects of its normative operations—not failings, but the more complete and thorough implementation of the existing social order, an automated system of injustice. Contemporary attempts to ratify the flexible relationships of 'the social' into fixed privileges, (not only via the rule of law, but via the autonomous and automated systems of computers), are products of the social, political, and economic instabilities/uncertainties created by technological change; expanding how 'the social' has been conceived historically to integrate new technologies of communication and relations does not alter its foundations, even if it changes their expression.[46] Automating the maintenance of "social identity" and privilege via "social credit" for all classes only superficially provides a corrective to the socio-political threat of expansions to the 'society of leisure'—replacing the complexity of human social dynamics with digital systems of control reassures those in positions of cultural authority of their continued dominance.

The fantasy that automating social systems currently expressed by humans is a way to eliminate the bias contained in 'the social' and thereby produce 'justice' is an fallacy that refuses to acknowledge that machine learning does not eliminate bias, but simply amplifies existing biases in the data used to train the system. This translation of 'the social' into instrumentalities enables new types of valorization that inevitably expand into previously unvalorized domains within 'the social'; AI is of immanent concern, not simply as a determinant issue of magnified bias, but also reflexively, as a transformation of human society driven by demands for new sources of value and the challenges posed through the fantasy of automation itself.

"Art and culture" conceived as an ever-expanding realm of spectacles and experiences allows this explicit colonization of 'the social' by mechanisms of societal control, such as AI, that primarily maximize valorization.[47] The advertising-centric model of information distribution employs pervasive monitoring to increase profit from advertising sales by exploiting social distinctions and divisions, i.e. differences of *identity*: these developments are not a demonstration of conspiratorial actions, but are instead collateral effects of how AI facilitates emotional responses as a mechanism to increase individual engagement in media via both a selective presentation of information to human audiences, and the limited sets of options made available to them. The more clearly polarized the resulting segmentation is, the more readily it can be subjected to valorization.

Dissolving traditional conceptions of "art and culture" into personal experiences illustrates how AI has enabled "behavioral stylometry" to manipulate *identity* into rigidly defined and opposing positions, which continues the use of agnotology to thwart political opposition to the expansive valorization of digital capitalism.[48] This instrumentality modulates the autonomous editorial decisions about what to show to whom that reinforces the capture of *identity* and its role in the contemporary extension of the definition of "art and culture" to include *any* social activity, abetted by the shift from capital as 'repository of value' to capital as a 'title to future production.'

To ignore this reciprocity and entanglement of AI with the social order that produces it is the aura of the digital. The expectation that automation will eliminate all of society's flaws, biases, and lapses masks how the heritage of colonial rule, inequities of social order, disparate access to economic opportunities, and unequal applications of law or criminal justice are all dimensions of human society that have always existed, and have always required conscious redress.

The anti-democratic tendencies enabled by the translation of 'the social' into the instrumentality of AI and the creation of the *PAZ* are paralleled by this technology's potential to reveal structural and systemic biases. By demonstrating areas of unrecognized or unacknowledged injustice, AI provides opportunities to develop solutions that do not replicate the grievances of the past by shifting harm from one group to another by revealing *how* the colonial foundations of bias (such as racism, sexism, homophobia, and religious intolerance) are still operative dimensions of 'the social'; however, this potential use for machine learning demands careful examination and human legislative oversight. It is not something that can be produced by fiat, no matter how well intentioned. Addressing injustices produced by these autonomous systems first requires accepting that *the biases these systems automate are structural features of the society that produces them.* AI will amplify existing bias unless their training data is carefully calibrated and corrected before the system's use, otherwise AI may cause injustices to be exacerbated. The social acceptance of past harms this process requires may be an insurmountable obstacle because employing AI systems as a mechanism to locate and minimize injustice requires acknowledging that bias is not a malfunction or problem in their programming. Injustice is a reflection of how human society is unjust; machine learning isolates and amplifies what is already occurring. The inclusion of biases, prejudices, and deficiencies in AI is inevitable; addressing them is an issue for regulatory and legislative action since they are a reflection of inherently social and cultural grievances.

The fantasy of automation thus reveals its Janus nature, offering an emancipation from the drudgery of determinative and rote labor, while simultaneously destabilizing wealth as a proxy for social status and position. As AI displaces agency, intention becomes more important for 'the social' even as it becomes problematic: the authority to demand production commence is never a neutral activity, devoid of contingent and arbitrary demands: the prerogatives of social status are linked to expectations for *identity,* and the allowances made for agency within those confines are subject to continuous monitoring and valorization by digital systems and AI—data that is the commodity produced by immaterial facture, complementing its use in machine learning and bespoke productions that shape public opinion and 'engineer' society-level outcomes. These relationships entangle "behavioral stylometry" with the operations of surveillance::agnotology as ubiquitous control systems that pervade 'the social' in digital capitalism, and which AI accentuates, transforming them into a systemic, unaccountable apparatus that the *PAZ* attempts to move beyond legal redress. This crisis arises from the extension of the 'society of leisure' that erases a signifier of privilege: if wealth is no longer a reflection of an individual's morality, exception, or position in society, then the edifice constructed around those distinctions to defend industrialism from its detractors also implodes.

Capitalism depends on emblematic transfers, which derive from Enlightenment concerns with agency, apparent in how nineteenth century industrialization viewed all human labor as a highly specialized type of machinery. This ideology anticipates the twentieth century dominance of the assembly line where human labor operates as the minimally intelligent linkages between processes which truncate and isolate human agency into rote actions. This productive technology reduces the translation of instructions through a human intermediary by assigning disparate, unthinking actions to labor, a devaluing of labor's intelligence that continues to shape the accelerating pace of AI deployment.[49] Yet these impacts will not be primarily economic because 'the social' responds to transformations of human labor in ways that reflect how the disruption of societal hierarchies are the primary concern, rather than economic displacements or their impacts on labor, which are often invisible: for example, automated systems that generate news stories from data—such as the results of a sporting event, or weather coverage—do so without their human audience even noticing. These systems have reduced the number of journalists needed, and changed the work required from those who still perform these tasks, reflecting the capacity to automate complex, but rote intelligent decisions that historically have required human labor.

Those who have privileges invariably seek ways to hold on to them and maintain their status within society. Historical alignments of human agency, class position, and social standing with the disposition of agency are apparent in the inferior position, low social status, and lack of esteem granted to both manual and affective labor. When a worker's agency is put in service of another, alien mind that directs them without requiring any intellectual contribution, their status as "human" is diminished. A simplistic reversal of values—that in a world of universal *leisure*, *work* becomes a social signifier of status—is a misconception of how agency converges on the societal hierarchy: to surrender one's agency to another is a dehumanizing subservience. To imagine a simple reversal is to misapprehend the problem.

Structural changes to capitalist production created by AI directly impact labor and influence those ideologies separating *idleness* and *leisure* that were essential to industrial production. The invention of "labor saving" machines belongs to a lineage that begins with the emancipation of forced labor (serfdom) and its replacement by progressively more regimented forms of production culminating in the industrial revolution; yet the conversion of agency into a commodity and its role in the creation of value serves to alienate agency from labor, concentrating it into the reflective judgments of managerial decisions.[50] The expansion of the 'society of leisure' that industrialism produced necessitated a re-imagining of *time* in relation to the industrial order that was maintained by the willingness of labor to remain within the factory. The utopian aspirations for a reduced work week made possible by improvements in efficiency prophesied in the 1930s have failed to emerge, not because productivity did not increase, but because new technologies—and the new expertise they required—shifted the roles for agency, but did not alter the necessity for that agency in production. Increased efficiencies did not result in a general elevation of the mass human population into the 'society of leisure.'

The replacements of labor offered by AI systems—whether shifting workers into *leisure* or *idleness*—will force a reckoning with how non-productive time is conceived. These conflicts are all expressions of differential status attached to human agency and its refraction throughout 'the social.' The uses of autonomous agency (AI) are an expression of cultural concerns with human agency and the translation of differentials in the societal hierarchy into the productive, political, and financial dimensions of capitalist development that demands *leisure* be a privilege of the dominant social classes, and establishes the opposition between *idleness* and *leisure* as a class differentiator, a signifier of status within the social hierarchy. The gradual expansion of *leisure* in the twentieth century conceived it as a time of consumption that asserts social status and position explicitly through conspicuous displays of 'waste' (nonproductive) activity that depend on displays of wealth.

Idleness, like sloth and indolence, is a negative form of agency in which action is held in a state of suspension, not as a reflection of an exalted social status and position, but rather in a demonstration of a failing or a lack of social standing that is typically connected to poverty, immorality, and unemployment. Technological unemployment demonstrates the low social status and position of *idleness* in the forced inaction of workers, their becoming surplus to requirements. *Idleness* is not chosen but imposed, a stark opposition to the activity of *leisure,* which is defined by freedom from the demands of work and labor. The conflation of inactivity with *idleness* by the lower classes is a resentiment of historical class distinctions that serves as a social impediment to any potential 'society of leisure,' suggesting it is immoral and alienating.

Where *leisure* for elites often includes art (and cultural pursuits), the 'expanded leisure' of the middle classes (immaterial laborers) is more commonly conceived as a form of consumptive valorization; expansions of *leisure* will likely accentuate class differences to avoid the "social identity threat" produced by a massive expansion to the 'society of leisure.' Competition for social status and position is a type of valorized self-display, already emergent with the economy of "influencers" on social media, that derives from the extent to which someone's actions are "broadcast" widely to a human audience. Automation is central to this development, making its role in this new social order apparent by how it ruptures the role of *leisure* as non-production.

Distinctions of *idleness* and *leisure* maintain established dimensions of social status and position (reinforced by *identity*) that come to demarcate hieratic position and replicate Descartes' separation of *mind* (reflective judgment) and *body* (determinative labor), giving different social status to each half of the pair. These relations are categorical. *Body* is always associated with socially disenfranchised groups, apparent in the essentialism that considers women only as reproductive bodies, as well as the racist status of slaves and indigenous populations conceived as irrelevant, disposable workers: as critic Hito Steryl has noted,"brutal violations of bodily integrity such as genital mutilation, the immolation of widows, bride sale, or domestic violence are made socially acceptable as customs and traditions by means of cultural concepts. Crime is normalized as culture."[51] The importance of moralistic judgment as a justification for dehumanizing labor—whether as "housework" or "care giving" performed by women, or as the conditions of factory workers generally—is reflected in the nineteenth century assumption that the productive, 'uniform labor' of industrial capitalism is poor, unskilled, uneducated, and unsophisticated.[52]

This capitalist ideology, when ascendent, was not universally embraced. Moralizing challenges to industrialization emerged along side the first modern factories in the eighteenth century; by the middle of the nineteenth century, Romanticism had become a cultural revolt against the machine and its products. Agency (intent) is central to this debate. The labor unionization movement, design reform movements (such as William Morris's Arts and Crafts Movement, as well as Art Nouveau, and Jugendstyl or Secession), and Marxism are all critical responses to industrialism whose demands for the increased mobility of raw materials, production, and commodities made possible by improvements in technology, transportation, and infrastructure has created a global wage arbitrage. These shifts in production between countries exploit the lower costs and differential legal allowances, recreating a similar arbitrage that emerged in the United States during the late nineteenth century in response to the development of rail lines. The mid-twentieth century developments of shipping containers and global shipping networks affirm these nineteenth century developments as a continuation of historical colonialism that dominates the contemporary logistics of production; however, the dependence of this global system on human social activity—the identification of *utility*—establishes the centrality of *leisure* to the "autonomous capitalism" that the fantasy of automation suggests.

The emergence of digital capitalism in the 1990s—evident in the drive towards surveillance (pervasive monitoring), financialization, and automation (AI)—renders the transformative impacts of *leisure* on social life as questions of class, justice, and freedom, but expressed via consumption choices within the marketplace because commodities lacking *use value* cannot be valorized. Associating *identity* with *leisure* and *luxury* creates *use value* (*utility*) for those activities and productions—such as media entertainments—that have a central role in the maintenance of existing hierarchies and social coherence. Parasocial relationships and "fandom" are expressions of *identity* even as they create new opportunities for value extraction. The demographic emergence of siloed group identities isolated within their own spheres of agreement increasingly replaces marketing to common or shared interests; digital automation has been crucial to these transformations of audience engagement, and AI systems make their bespoke customization and valorization commonplace.

The differentials between the valuation of what are increasingly immaterial commodities, their protection against appropriation, and the convergence between those types of labor that were systematically devalued in the assembly line with the new types of intelligent (skilled) labor demanded in immaterial production reinstate the same instrumental ignorance apparent in the operations of machine learning and autonomous agency that converge on intellectual labor which does not invent new rules or approaches: philosopher Immanuel Kant's unintentional (coincidental) 'anticipation' of AI could not be more explicit. Machine learning employs what he termed 'determinative judgments' in his book *Critique of Pure Reason*; any human labor that can be abstracted into a fixed set of predetermined rules can be automated:

> Determinative judgment [always operates] under universal transcendental laws given by the understanding, is only subsumptive. The law is marked out for it a priori, and hence it does not need to devise a law

> of its own so that it can subsume the particular in nature under the universal.[53]

Kant's 'determinative judgment' presages on Ruskin's discussion of human labor in the factory and the particular decisions that define subjective thought. The dualistic separation of managerial and productive labor reifies this separation between "human" and "automated tool" that defines the cultural insignificance of intellectual labor which matches outcomes to *a priori* knowledge; it is dismissed by 'the social' as belonging to the same realm as other types of industrial production. However, the distinction between industrialism that renders thought as a mechanical process (assembly line) and its automation by machinery (AI) demonstrates how the rote 'technical judgment' still requires human agency (as *utility*) to produce *value*.

The transformative effect of the digital on rote intelligent labor, no matter how complex or specialized,[54] has already altered labor intensive industries such as typesetting or animation, making complex and formerly difficult/expensive types of production commonplace: to print a single page of letters and images required approximately one week's labor by skilled craftsmen for Johannes Gutenberg when he invented his press in the fifteenth century; today documents such as a page of search results are immediately available, and do not require human action beyond making the request for their production. The documents are entirely machine-generated. The images, text, and layout all organized automatically without human oversight by using rote templates, and the text displayed, as well as its images, are sourced from within a database of material that was collected autonomously. What was once the product of highly trained, skilled human labor becomes instead a commodity product, generally available on-demand,

and requiring no special skill or training to access. What was once rarified, valuable, specialized labor has become common, worthless, disposable. The site of valorization has shifted from the "content" on display and the creation of the templates themselves—the ur-design employed—to the act of requesting the document. While the result of a "web search" may not seem like a significant artistic creation, nor even a product of intelligent labor, prior to the digital computer merely collating the information presented on such a page required significant human labor and expertise, just as typesetting that information and printing it for display were also labor intensive tasks requiring high degrees of technical skill. The very mundaneness of this task is an indication of how rapidly 'the social' accommodates the displacement of rote human labor in tasks without high social standing. These factors congeal into the roles, activities, and beliefs that define groups—each *identity* serves to sort social relationships into hieratic positions—and then enfranchises *leisure* as a class privilege.

The protocols for machine learning demand an unmoving and immobile framework where decisions about its application are always determined in advance. Kant explains that these self-directed refinements of existing knowledge are innate aspects of self-definition understood as a question of freedom, of human agency bounded by the *a priori* horizons of possibility that are dictated by culture:

> The first alternative [to understand judgment] is rational and mathematical cognition through construction of the concept; the second is mere empirical (mechanical) cognition, which can never yield necessary and apodictic propositions. Thus I could indeed dissect my empirical concept of gold, and would gain from this nothing more than the ability to

> enumerate everything that I actually think in connection with this word; but although a logical improvement would thus occur in my cognition, no increase or addition would be gained in it.[55]

Kant's limitations on reflective judgments, and their separation from 'rational and mathematical cognition,' anticipates how questioning *who* is allowed reflective agency reveals the issue of *identity* is central to the generative activity produced by the 'rational and mathematical cognition' that defines machine learning. The unintelligence of this system makes the flaws of human society obvious because it does not instrumentalize the idiosyncratic and subjective modifiers that humans use to alter and adjust the application of rules: in being transformed into data, all actions are rendered equivalent. AI grants human agency only the limited the degrees of freedom offered by the design of the system itself. Technology instrumentalizes the role of culture in dominating this expressive "space."

Questioning whose *identity* is linked to the mind (reflective judgment) and whose to the body (determinative judgment) reveals access to *leisure* is an expression of class, gender, generational wealth, and educational attainment. Ironically, Romanticism assumes this ideology of determinative versus reflective as the unquestionable basis to separate the human from the machine. The conception of 'work' as productive labor typical of industrial capitalism—the agency hired from labor for a wage—is central to *identity* in capitalism, acting to suppress the role of *leisure* as a form of self-expression; at the same time, and perhaps more dramatically, the role of *leisure* is a class distinction, a 'waste' that is reserved only for those whose labor is not valued in 'hours worked,' but by the nature of their mental activity. The fantasy of automation reinforces existing class bias by transforming human labor into something akin to mindless machines even for those seeking to emancipate it from that status: Ruskin and the Romantics create a self-fulfilling prophesy for labor. Autonomous agency continues these ideological divisions within 'the social,' accentuating and reanimating historical denigrations of determinative labor: the low status individual is an exemplar of their group/class *identity* (determinative), while the elite individual is always unique, an exemplar of only their self (reflective). These recurring and repeating associations of mind/reflection/human and body/determination/machine are cultural ideologies that focus and constrain personal and group *identity* equally.[56]

For the Enlightenment, the expression/creation that is *identity* is an act of *self-definition* via the exercise of agency essential to *being-human*. When rendered as an aesthetic theory—*formalism*—it articulates the essential nature of Modernist aesthetics through a process of ascetic reduction that eliminates all the intrusions of hybrid, foreign, and alien ideation in an assertion of the colonial difference between the imperial center and the provincial margins. It attempts to remove all that is determinative from the reflective act. The American art critic Clement Greenberg explains this protocol of aesthetic refinement as a specifically "Modernist ontology" via a proposal of 'purity' that links agency, *identity*, aesthetics (art) and the colonial enterprise together, producing a reinforcing matrix of racism, sexism, and exceptionalism that masks capitalist valorization:

> The essence of Modernism, as I see it, lies in the use of characteristic methods of a discipline to criticize the discipline itself, not in order to subvert it but in order to entrench it more firmly in its area of competence. Kant used logic to

establish the limits of logic, and while he withdrew much from its old jurisdiction, logic was left all the more secure in what there remained to it.[57]

Human agency is the Enlightenment's irreducible dimension of being-human that allows the pursuit of something anticipating the noumenal. Aesthetic Modernism affirms these claims[58] by attempting to recover a primal state of purity[59] through abstract art: Alfred Jarry's *pataphysics* which parodies scientific procedures, or in Marcel Duchamp's *chance operations* where the only "chance" element is the essential intervention of human agency to interpret a mechanistic result,[60] and in Surrealism's appropriation of psychology as an irrational, creative protocol.[61] Contemporary Glitch Art explicitly connects these transcendental aesthetics to the misfunctions of digital technology.[62] These aesthetics continue the Romantic attempt to 're-enchant the world' by rejecting rationalism, industrialism, and empirical science—expressions of the ideological attempt to counter those aspects of industrialism that challenge traditional social, political, and cultural orders. Aesthetic form assumes a distinctly social function as an expression of the moral superiority which accompanies any elevated status in this ideology that perversely denies art has any role in 'the social.'

Greenberg's "Modernist ontology" reveals how this *a priori* fundamentalism defines /art/, guides its application, and demonstrates how determinative choices limit and constrain the results of their application in advance—his formalist argument converges on the restrictions of labor's agency in industrialism; it provides an aesthetic analogue to the moral argument of the 'Protestant Work Ethic.' The *a priori* ratification of outcomes by Modernist art and industrialism parallel the instrumentalization of outcomes via machine learning: those criteria employed in production reflect cultural biases, as the formalist manifesto "Ornament and Crime" (1909) by Austrian architect Adolph Loos demonstrates:

> The child is amoral. To us the Papuan is also amoral. The Papuan slaughters his enemy and devours them. He is no criminal. If, however, the modern man slaughters and devours somebody, he is a criminal or a degenerate. The Papuan tattoos his skin, his boat, his oar, in shore, everything that is within his reach. He is no criminal. The modern man who tattoos himself is a criminal or a degenerate. There are prisons where eighty percent of the inmates bear tattoos. Those who are tattooed but are not imprisoned are latent criminals or degenerate aristocrats. If a tattooed person dies at liberty, it is only that he died a few years before he committed a murder. [...] The man of our time who daubs the walls with erotic symbols to satisfy an inner urge is a criminal or a degenerate. It is obvious that his [primitive] urge overcomes man: such symptoms of degeneration most forcefully express themselves in public conveniences. One can measure the culture of a country by the degree to which its lavatory walls are daubed.[63]

Loos' early proposal of *formalism* draws together racism, colonialism, and capitalist production in an attempt to sever the cultural association of skilled production with morality and aesthetic quality[64] by opposing the performative demonstration of skill by the skilled worker (decoration). He would deny any expression of reflective agency by labor because reflective agency is a class privilege, reserved for the direction of labor—workers are simply to "mechanically" perform the prescribed actions without question or input. His argument for savings in greater efficiency and reduced wages resulting from a reduction in complexity allows factories to produce more commodities without needing the highly skilled workers *who are more expensive to employ*. These arguments for formalism mirror those made in support of the assembly line, automated machinery, and contemporary AI systems. His aesthetic argument to replace the craftsman's agency in favor of managerial agency disguises its economic benefit by making a moral claim whose colonialism is self-evident in the conflation of "immorality" with the behaviors of what were regarded as "primitive" societies in 1909, suggesting the adoption of these behaviors is a contamination of the Modern by the Primitive. The formalist elimination and restriction his manifesto proposes would prevent this corruption.

Formalist distinctions separate the dominant people (Europeans) from those inhabiting their colonial possessions (Papuans). By rendering a "Papuan" equivalent to a child, Loos robs them of their agency and culture; it is a blatantly racist formulation extended to include anyone in Loos's own society who differs from his ideology: to disagree or challenge his proposal would be a demonstration of the immorality he opposes. Claiming his economic argument as a moral position—an ascetic denial of eroticism and the body—enables the agency of the 'Modern man' who rejects decoration to be fundamentally better from that of the serf or manual laborer, and separates them from the less-than-human peoples their empires conquered: connections between industrial workers and colonized or enslaved peoples simultaneously justifies their dehumanization as morally correct, creating a self-reinforcing system of social status and position expressed by the aesthetics of commodity production.

Colonial beliefs about whose *identity is* superior emerge as the Modernist emphasis on "ontology" that Post-Modernism criticized but failed to replace:

racism, sexism, nationalism, and homophobia (creating proposals such as eugenics) all produce acceptable and unacceptable types of *identity* that are linked to more than merely social behaviors, but include ethnicity, aesthetics, morality—all very different from art, even antithetical to the ideology of creativity, but they are all responses to the same "social identity threats" posed by cultural change and the extension of privileges and rights. The proposition of achieving any type of 'purity' depends on which features are considered essential in an expression of social status and position.

Both Greenberg and Loos link art, morality, industrialism, and cultural otherness to the economics of facture and the role of agency, but these implicitly racist, classist, and Eurocentric dimensions of formalist aesthetics are not necessarily obvious from any consideration of Modernist art. Loos' statements about degeneracy and criminality as absolute and inescapable features of *identity* link his claims to the ontological status of the individual. The consolidation of roles made possible by these formalist aesthetics enables separations between the commodity's conception and the productive labor of facture, a distinction that promotes the standardization apparent in the uniform definitions of distance, movement, location that are fundamental to the infrastructures of industrial production and colonialism, and which 'purity' in art tries to replicate. Without the uniformity of these implicit managerial structures, the operative advantages of logistics cannot operate—the globalized flows of information, raw material, and commodity production they orchestrate—and the efficiencies made possible by AI become irrelevant. All these technologies of dominance belong to the same lineage as Greenberg's "Modernist ontology" for art. These self-reinforcing cultural beliefs enable automation and the autonomous agency of AI to continue the cultural influence of these hidden dimensions of Modernism into the Contemporary. They are significant because the implementation of machine learning assumes a more sinister disposition as this 'moralistic ontology' is instrumentalized by the 'Technology Platform for Social Intervention' (*TPSI*) and the automation of social status and position by "start-up societies" such as *Próspera.* Every organizational technology, once institutionalized, becomes difficult to dethrone. While the abundance of industrial facture and digital replication is neither uniformly nor equitably distributed, capitalism's rationalized production consolidates this hidden 'moralistic ontology' under a managerial ideology that defends privilege rather than produces justice. Digital technology holds the colonial nature of this construction in place since it has become essential not only to the flow of physical material, but to both immaterial labor and the data it generates. Instrumental cultural values become a technology that hides its ideological foundations and their radical displacement of distance and importance within the automated systems themselves—the Janus-face of the fantasy of automation—not as bias, but in their operative function as a system of social regimentation, surveillance, valorization administered by automated systems that block human oversight.

The aura of the digital governs these ideological fantasies of direct control over production as a paradoxical freedom from having to perform manual, degrading labor implicit in the Modernist lineage. It justifies the disemployment of labor by AI for tasks that were formerly the exclusive domain of human activity.[65] As automation colonizes 'the social' and valorizes *identity,* social relationships become a reflection of *potential value* that emerges from AI enabling autonomous production and the marketing of *leisure* and *luxury* to increasingly narrow audiences who employ them as mechanisms for subjective self-expression (*identity*), closing the tautology. This combination is toxic: reflective judgment is neutralized by valorization via the bespoke, on-demand facture the digital accentuates, highlights, and maintains as *identity* within the database.

Surveillance is central to converting *identity* into a digital commodity—this changed function for *identity* inverts the relationships between *value* and *use value* theorized by Marx,[66] bringing all those elements he called "metaphysical" and dependent on *utility* into dominance; aesthetics is prominent among these values. *Potential values* created by semiotic facture are neither productive labor nor resources expended, as in historical types of facture, but instead depend on activations of *desires* within their human audience to be realized as *value,* thus exacerbating the fundamental crisis that accompanies the maintenance and oversight of 'intellectual property' by pervasive monitoring and digital rights management. The fantasy of automation enables this valorized *leisure* to transform *identity* into a narcissistic imaginary that purely and exclusively engages with the reflective judgments which are the domain of the highest social strata. It reinforces demands for automation, while at the same time denying the role of human agency and labor in implementing those aspirations. Attempts to contain *leisure* within this prescribed and determinate set of operations acts to ratify it as a class privilege, *luxury*,[67] simultaneously creating barriers to the 'society of leisure.' These reflections of traditional beliefs about the necessity and morality of labor demonize inactivity as *idleness* to justify maintaining the societal hierarchy that emerged with sustenance farming.

The 'society of leisure' is a mirage, always just out of reach—both the reward and the result of distancing agency from the mundane necessity of rote activities that implement the managerial dictum—but the aspiration to expand and extend *leisure* throughout the societal hierarchy is not entirely a fallacy (changes in technology and production do enable more groups to participate); thus this aspiration cannot be unmasked as a lie. Irrational concerns with social status and hierarchal position evoke a manifest destiny that directs activity and action (and disenfranchises human agency) but can not be accounted along traditional lines of rational interrogation, evidence, or logic—they are affective labor mediated by agnotology, and administered by automation. Although this ideology is empirically grounded in lived experience, much like the immaterialism that informs the aura of the digital itself, its hypothetical progression leads to a corrupting influence of fantasy which becomes new opportunities for social capture, valorization, and accumulation without concern for remuneration. This unpaid form of productive action managed and administered by autonomous systems introduces contingent and capricious factors into objective determinations of *value*.

The 'moralistic ontology' that Modernist "purity" signifies (both for art and in social relations) emerges in that instrumentalization which renders the decisions of its builders—whether explicitly as a function of the programming, or implicitly as a product of biases in the training data—as reifications of a social order that constrains questions of self-definition to only those dimensions that serve valorization processes. The role of 'purity' in the Modernist development of industrial capitalism (which reaches an apogee with the assembly line) is a logical necessity for the digital's attempts to simplify (figuratively and literally) aesthetic, cultural, social, and political relationships—expressed by the priority for increased efficiency in industrial facture. AI transforms Kant's determinative judgements into active constraints on human agency by removing the functional opposition that is always a potential for labor that must perform a task, replacing it with rote operations.

In rendering *identity* as a commodity, AI protocols constrain human expression through the mutually reinforcing impacts of a feedback between the machine and the actions of its operators that incorporates the collateral impacts that these systems pose for interactions with human society. Art's 'moralistic ontology' affirms or ratifies the colonial designation of certain populations as 'impure' and thus essentially problematic and requiring control; operations which the use of AI reiterates in a closed loop affirming traditional social hierarchies. Those options offered by digital systems rapidly become the only options considered or available, even though social status and position is a performative relationship cued by *inter alia* race, gender, ethnicity, and language as well as through factors such as property and dress that are also constrained by economics. This network of prescribed *a priori* potentials differentiates the fixity of AI from human agency and social expressions of position and hierarchy. The importance of understanding capitalism anthropologically, as a system of unequal social distribution, could not be more obvious; 'wealth' provides a proxy for those displays of social status and position which the democratic expansions of bespoke production (*luxury*) and the extension of *leisure* equally subvert.

Modernism advanced a 'moralistic ontology' in support of a repressive system whose injustice was self-evident, and which returns in the uses and implementation of AI as a defence against change—as a justification for that which cannot be justified. Democratic expansions of what were formerly privileges claimed by the elite are disruptive. Those changes in access, visibility, or exclusiveness for proxy signifiers assumes the appearance of a loss of status to those who already enjoy them (creating a "social identity threat") precisely because when the distinguishing features that mark difference disappear, the automatic assumption of social status they confer also vanishes. The historical alignment of these factors informs the question of *agency* that defines the separation between the fine arts and the creative design, a distinction effaced by the fantasy of automation. But when all debased tasks of low status are automated, their elimination does not guarantee an expansion of the 'society of leisure' or the status accruing to historical elites being extended to labor following the automation of their tasks—to do so is unquestionably the greatest "social identity threat" posed by democracy, new technology, and the end of colonialism. AI performing labor that historically required human intelligence does not guarantee an expansion of privilege that coincides with the spread of democratic ideals and traditions in society. Those populations performing tasks which were of low social prestige will likely remain at the same low level within the societal hierarchy in a betrayal of the promise offered by industrialization and the capacity to create abundance.

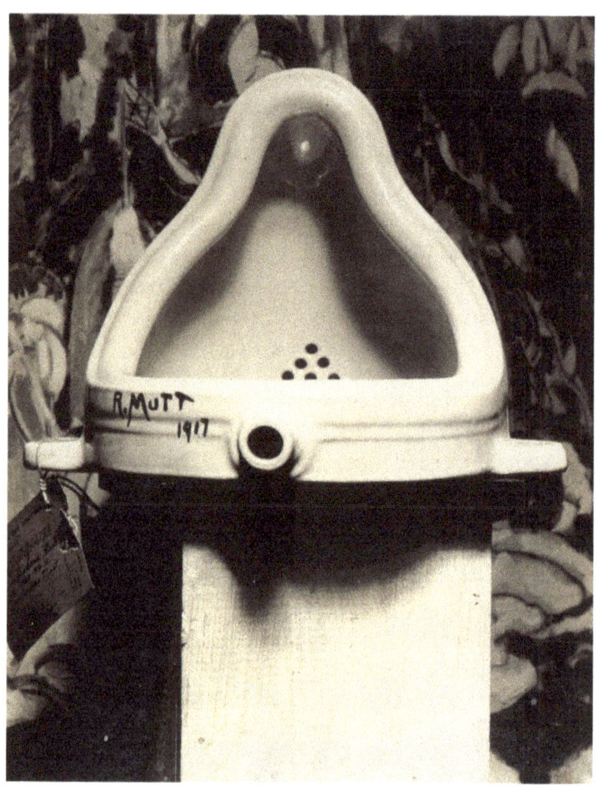

Figure 4: *Fountain* (1917) by "R. Mutt" (Marcel Duchamp), published in *The Blind Man* no. 2, 1917. This image of a photocomposite is composed from ~12 photographs by Alfred Stieglitz that were collaged into an assemblage by Duchamp before being rephotographed for publication.

The societal hierarchy is the apparatus expressed through status display, and art is *the* status display par excellence.[68] This recognition brings the historical linage of art into direct confrontation with the capitalist valorization of culture through the dual dependencies of [1] the constraints of precedent on aesthetic evaluation (*conventionality*) evident in how the audience identifies art from their past experiences,[69] and [2] the requirement for human engagement (*utilization*) that activates art as a multifaceted expression (*use value*).[70] Automation intervenes in these social relationships to draw attention to the role of *identity* in the apprehension of the art object itself, revealing a convergence between the 'law of automation' (anything that can be automated will be) and the aesthetic problems of autonomous agency (via both weak and strong AI equally).

[1] Human agency is central to the identification of aesthetic objects and their status within /art/, as Marcel Duchamp's readymade *Fountain* (1917) [Figure 4] demonstrates by appearing to offer only a limited role for human agency, a limitation that brings the 'intentional function' (ascriptions of artistic agency to artwork) into consciousness as a contingent phenomenon.[71] Contemporary digital art follows this trajectory that began with photography and continued in the historical avant-garde's critique of traditional, metaphysical concerns with art making, articulated by collector Louise Norton in her essay "The Richard Mutt Case" defending Duchamp's *Fountain*:

> Whether Mr. Mutt [Duchamp] with his own hand made the fountain or not has no importance. He CHOSE it. He took an ordinary article of life, placed it so that its useful significance

> disappeared under the new title and point of view—created a new thought for that object.[72]

That *Fountain* resembles an industrially produced porcelain object is apt. Norton describes an aesthetic not based in facture, but still reliant on the agency of the artist, arguing that the only agency which matters is the reflective judgment (intent) that decides what the /art/ will be, mirroring the importance of choice by the photographer and anticipating the role of the artist confronting AI—the fantasy of automation attenuates these links between human action and artistic production. This argument suggests that productive action (determinative judgement implementing the reflective design) is irrelevant to aesthetics and art.

An identical challenge to agency in art is posed by Maurizio Cattelan's *Comedian* (2019), a banana duct taped to a gallery wall: the production of the work does not correspond to its aesthetic status, which derives from the audience's consciousness of its significance and intertextual relationships to earlier art (such as *Fountain*). Both works divide the audience into two groups of unequal social status and position: *those who understand* what's happening in the art and *those who do not*. The separation of human agency from the production of the work that Norton emphasizes—the act of *choosing* the object—displaces art production from the agency that sets facture in motion, anticipating the bespoke productions made possible by AI that potentially offer the same *luxury* which has been historically limited only to elites to a much larger audience, undermining the *exclusivity* of these productions as signifiers of social status.

Both art objects announce the *use value* of their aesthetics explicitly as a proxy for position within the societal hierarchy; they are a sorting apparatus—the *utility* of art that defines its *use value* is to separate class and be a marker for distinctions of social identity and position. This intentionality is not limited to the expensive or exclusive products of the art world, but applies equally to all aesthetic productions, whether fabricated as bespoke objects or as industrial commodities. The audience's response to the aesthetic object distinguishes their position within the societal hierarchy in a direct expression of *utility* that parallels art's other significances. The same specialized knowledge that produces art is required to understand it, no matter its form: shared aesthetics unify disparate groups (subcultures)[73] that collect and display art as factions within the "creative class."[74] Art provides a mechanism of distinction belying claims for aesthetic contemplation as a pursuit open to all classes; art is thus a token that evokes "social identity threat."

Social functions are not automatable: they are independent of the work and its particular aesthetic features, being instead expressions of relations within 'the social,' not empirical features of form. Unlike traditional valorization processes, the *use value* of aesthetics produces the art object's *exchange value*, rather than issues of scarcity, labor, or facture: it connects the reflective judgments that are conventionally separated from determinative activities as the *use value* of art. *Utility* is created by *exclusivity*, then displayed by *leisure* and *luxury* as they converge on *identity*. Anthropological approaches to aesthetics bridge the commonplace function of *identity* as a unique identifier with its symbolic understanding as a transcendent value expressed via aesthetic form that provides an empirical referent (*utility*) for what are metaphysical dimensions of human culture. Art valuations are not an issue of production, but derive from within the metaphysical values of *utility,* hidden by an ideology claiming that class position and privilege are *not* constraints on aesthetic importance. Transfers from *utility* into *exchange value* happen in art as a valorization of its capacity—both realized and potential—to serve as a proxy for social status and position, illuminating connections between what are the otherwise incommensurate spheres of *exchange value* and *use value.*[75]

Digital capitalism involves a transformation of traditionally interpersonal affects that have been the *substance* of aesthetic significance since the advent of the Modernist avant-garde in the nineteenth century[76] into opportunities for expanded profit extraction as the societal hierarchy becomes merely a contingency awaiting valorization (the function of *luxury*). These engagements with *identity* via aesthetics correspond to the propositions of an irrational marketplace where decisions are expressions of social identity: it requires the expansion of "culture." The *Culture Track* survey provides empirical evidence for these social transformations that increase the valorization of aesthetic work (art) by expanding which groups are included in its address, which then creates "social identity threats" (mollified by art consumption) as status becomes data within the matrix of surveillance and algorithmic management. In evacuating these historical separations between the elites and the serfs/slaves/factory workers or immaterial/manual laborers in the office, the hyperreal resulting from such developments collapses the historical use of art as a proxy for social status and position into a conflict that is not fundamentally concerned with wages or employment, but over the valorization of *identity* expressed through art, a reflection of the expanding 'society of leisure'; however, this new valorization of art and culture is problematic, not because it debases or even challenges /art/, but because it invents new status markers within 'the social.'

[2] The digital entangles social impacts with the aesthetic potentials of automation and AI by instrumentalizing aesthetics, as critic Robert Scott explains about artist Roxy Paine's mechanical implementation of Modernist formalism, in the process demonstrating these aesthetics on-going circulation in digital technology:

> Paine's *PMU* (Painting Manufacture Unit), 1999-2000 provides a perfect example of this rigorous engineering. [...] To make just one painting, the process [the machine follows] may repeat itself between 80 and 200 times, without any intervention whatsoever from the artist. [...] Paine's insistence on this technical exactitude and lack of superfluous detail reveals his surprisingly mechanistic understanding of the inventions he aptly regards as "labor saving devices." By automating processes lasting from may hours to many days, they spare the artist's time and attention, rendering his engaged presence irrelevant to the creation of the work.[77]

No human would make paintings like those resulting from the *PMU*—this process of art facture is purely mechanical—nevertheless, the art historical pedigree of these paintings is apparent through the formalist identification they instrumentalize: a blunt literalization of Clement Greenberg's demands for a materialist art. The paint has dribbled down the canvas, running off the bottom and leaving a fragile material fringe, while above is nothing but bare canvas. "What you see is what you see," but at the same time these recognitions and identifications depend entirely upon the audience's *a priori* knowledge of Modernist aesthetics. The PMU translates a rote formalism into the autonomous layering of paint where the artist's involvement becomes, if not attenuated, then entirely elided, yet perversely essential.

Paine's machine parodies claims that the anthropological aspects of art's social functions are irrelevant: its products simultaneously privilege a specific and implicit *identity* as the predicate of all its aesthetic functions. The reception and appreciation of these paintings is refractive of the social roles of *identity* that art manifests as separations distinguishing social position—class and educational attainment—of the audience encountering the work. These *identity* politics are only superficially absent from aesthetics since the hidden 'he' that is the white–cis–male–position–accepted–as–natural becomes explicit via Greenberg's "purification of each art"[78] that accentuates the *a priori* functions of class.

Although the *PMU* is not an AI system, its automation of the aesthetic process anticipates challenges emergent with works produced twenty years later via machine learning. The ideology of creativity illuminated by this digital system converges on historical debates over the aesthetic value and status of photography-as-art: this device instrumentalizes aesthetic judgment as an autonomous, predetermined protocol, fundamentally contradicting the historical, Enlightenment ideology of art and aesthetics as expressing reflective judgment. The *PMU* belongs to a lineage of art-making-machines which attenuate direct human action through the displacement of traditional craft and skill. This division between the creation of the artwork and the fabrication of that work responds to the same industrial demand for greater efficiency and precision balanced against production speed and fidelity that defined the assembly line. The increasing role of automation in this debate over agency (intention) in art emphasizes aesthetic questions that were formerly masked by the productive and material constraints of training and technique on artistic production: expressive significance, cultural embeddedness, and social utilization all entangle the identification of art with acts of human agency. Once the role of automation and AI enables an aesthetic construction independent of human agency, they become separate issues; the *PMU* thus anticipates the challenges to human agency posed by Pindar van Arman's AI software *CloudPainter* that performs a 'style transfer' between one artist and another (such as Pablo Picasso or Edvard Munch).[79] Because the *PMU's* automation and contemporary AI both displace the necessity of human agency, they resurrect and then exacerbate nineteenth century aesthetic problems introduced by the development of photography: the camera initializes a process of excision where the creative act that produced art became separable from human action; AI continues this lineage by attenuating and replacing human action and agency in art facture to unsettle questions that appeared resolved by the embrace of photography-as-art in the twentieth century.

The Enlightenment emphasis on determinative and reflective judgments provides the ideological foundation for this aesthetic debate over photography, evident in Ruskin's distinction of /art/ from capitalist production that separates managerial decisions about facture from the laborer's actions in performing those decisions. This traditional conception of aesthetics ratifies art as intentional (an expression of social status and position) paradoxically without acknowledging art's function as a proxy for status or position within the societal hierarchy.[80] This Modernist aesthetic heritage does not avoid issues of *use value*, but masks them by making the dimensions of semic analysis invisibly revelatory of educational attainment, social status, and position: *who* is looking is central to the interpretation of paintings made by the *PMU*, a dimension of their significance that manifests *identity* in the reception of the work by disguising its function as a sorting device. These paintings demonstrate how Contemporary aesthetics recenter the issue of human agency through the role of intertextual knowledge and interpretive expertise to establish the "object" itself as crucial to interpretation (especially when dematerialized by Conceptual Art), reinforcing its social function in the guise of aesthetic significance.

AI foregrounds this intentionality as a proxy for status and position. Replacing human labor with machinery follows a singular trajectory where the necessity for an intermediary, mediating, human agency constrained by technique is progressively attenuated, providing incompatible resolutions to the aesthetic problem posed by machines that either eliminates photography from being /art/ or redefines /art/ itself. Answering the question *'Is /art/ purely produced by the artist's intention (agency)?'* results in mutually exclusive potentials: either [yes] the rejection of non-human agency in the production of art, whether by AI or otherwise, legislating the particularity assigned to human agency via theories of *intentionalism*; or [no] a general redefinition of agency in relation to art, one that assimilates the critiques of *intentionalism* by focusing on the social and institutional framing for art.[81] Surprisingly, the expansion of art made by this aesthetic lineage (which includes inter alia *Fountain* and *Comedian,* as well as both photography and generative art) has remained within *intentionalism.* This understanding of the photographic camera's automated image production attenuates and elides the direct human action traditionally needed for image facture, but does not eliminate the role of human agency in directing (choosing) what appears in the photograph.[82] This accommodation of the photograph establishes the agency of the artist as the only factor in the creation

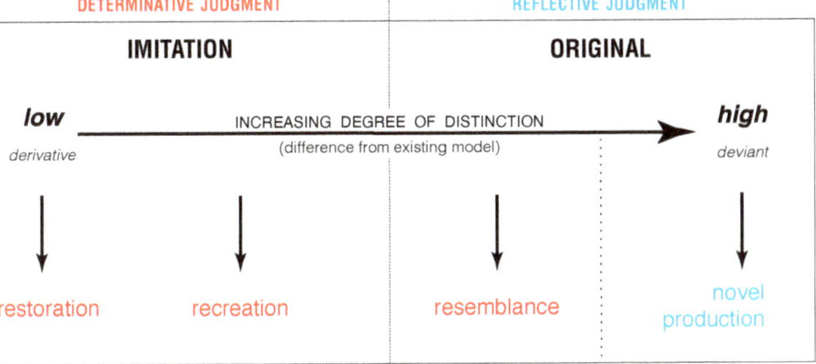

Figure 5: The range of aesthetic productions instrumentalized by autonomous systems and machine learning overlap with traditional aesthetic categories and appraisals, revealing their social function through the opposition between the social categories of 'art' and 'non-art.'

of the work that is significant to its production or articulation as-art—a role that is also asserted by *Fountain*.[83] In both these solutions, the *identity* of the artist is crucial to art's identification: knowledge about *who* the artist is determines the status as-art, and justifies art's exception from the typical concerns and understanding of capitalist production, placing /art/ in a different category of capitalist facture, "the cultural," that is evaluated separately from *exchange value.*

Conflicts over social identity are always immanent in art; this is the source of its "danger."

Art's cultural embeddedness derives from its social role as an expensive, rarified, scarce production (*luxury*). Figure 5 describes a range of interpretations for artistic agency (the separation between reflective and determinative judgments deployed to identify art objects) designating *original* and *imitation* works by their relationship to an *a priori* model. This taxonomy remains constant, whether the art is generated by machine or by hand. It diagrams concerns derived from nineteenth century aesthetics, apparent in the Arts and Crafts movement,[84] that emphasize the role of "autonomy" common to Modern, Post-Modern, and Contemporary art. This concept is essential to art's propositional *originality*,[85] and ironically articulates problems posed by artists making their own work. Aesthetic features such as 'style and form' characterizing an artist's work are emergent, unifying the art they make as *theirs*. All the recognitions that define *resemblance* necessarily complicate any *novel production* because self-similarity accompanies both categories of *original*. The distinction of *resemblance* versus *novel production* ultimately depends on audience beliefs about *prima causa*. The audience's beliefs about the *identity* responsible for the work justifies the identification as-art and so returns aesthetics to the questions of *exclusivity*—uniqueness, materiality, rarity—that define *luxury* commodities. These historical distinctions are always and only ever a social appraisal of the "moral right" to claim authorship, (enshrined by copyright, trademark, and patent law). It realizes the role of *utility* in this range by entangling the machine with the agency it displaces, reinforcing links between *identity* and *luxury* as aesthetics.

AI tends to circulate freely within this range as "non-art," obfuscating AI's art historical lineage that originates with the Modernist avant-gardes whose critiques of artistic virtuosity[86] amplify and demonstrate art's social functions. Although Conceptual Art attempts to divorce art from its aesthetic presentation, the recursive entanglement of 'rule setting' (reflective) and 'rule following' (determinative) defines *resemblance* in the reflective application of a determinative judgment: what AI renders as a rote system where human agency is neither a necessary nor sufficient condition of its ontology in a figurative dehumanization of art. Yet the requirement for human engagement (*utilization*) never vanishes, as Conceptual artist Sol LeWitt notes in his theoretical publication, *Sentences on Conceptual Art*:

> 17. All ideas are art if they are concerned with art and fall within the conventions of art.
> 18. One usually understands the art of the past by applying the conventions of the present, thus misunderstanding the art of the past.
> 19. The conventions of art are altered by works of art.
> 20. Successful art changes our understanding of the conventions by altering our perceptions.[87]

LeWitt's "conventions" are a determinative system that transforms all art objects into *resemblance*. The fantasy of automation is immanent in how Conceptual Art conceives immaterial (mental) labor as aesthetic software, limiting the ideology of creativity to only the reflective judgment of the artist in that plan's creation—digital technology instrumentalizes aesthetics, mirroring the role of *a priori* "design" common to other types of industrial facture, as in the paintings made by the *PMU*. This abstraction of aesthetic morphology and structure renders art from rote organizational instructions as Pindar van Arman's *CloudPainter* software does. Artistic "signature style" is a formal effect (as in a style manual for corporate identity[88])—demonstrating that determinative judgment is essential to aesthetic evaluation; thus a contradiction between determinative and reflective judgment inheres in the category of *resemblance*. While LeWitt's role for the artist in aesthetic production enunciates the

Modernist demand that art change "our understanding of the conventions," this apparatus separates human agency from the mechanical aspects of facture. This ambivalent shift produces a radical deskilling for art that parallels the industrial deskilling accelerated by the assembly line. AI belongs to this lineage that forces an acknowledgment that machine learning minimizes the *prima causa* of reflective judgment.

Connoisseurship is predicated on the problem *resemblance* presents for the category assignment /art/. "Conventions" do not resolve the paradox of reflective judgment becoming a determinative activity; they enable the automation of existing aesthetics as an instrumentality[89] that alters the role of human agency in facture without displacing the questions of social status and position that constrain the analysis of art: *luxury* always affirms elite *exclusivity*.[90] Any expansions of the audience for art create "social identity threats" addressed by Modernist denials of cultural significance and social function that mystify aesthetic perception by making it a class privilege; philosopher Kurt Rosinger demonstrates:

> The understanding of a work of art involves, for most men, not so much the enjoyment of its tones or colors or rhythmic movements and a comprehension and reaction to its underlying form, as it does an attempt to discover a hidden conceptual significance.[91]

Rosinger argues for "significant form" and against all other ways of seeing art. This formalist concern transforms aesthetics into an exceptional expression beyond the limits of 'the social' that allows the viewer to approach art as a numinous embrace of materiality. It evokes the 'moralistic ontology', which understands any concern with *utility* as a rejection of aesthetics, in a recapitulation of colonial bias. His argument fuses the phenomenology of the art object with appraisals of art as evidence for human agency (*intentionalism*) to imbue art with a transcendent character that erases its *utility* and any other meanings it may have—reflective judgment becomes irrelevant to the concerns of the critic–as–flâneur: "what you see is what you see." This art object conceived as a record of the artist's reflective engagements illuminates the ideology of creativity inscribed by Kant's distinctions between determinative and reflective judgments, which lead to a restrictive definition of aesthetic qualia via the role of *identity* (*intentionalism*) that cannot be avoided when confronting any art object.

AI's instrumentalization of aesthetics necessitates the expansion of audiences that is also demanded by digital capitalism's valorization processes. It elevates "art and culture" as performative activity—personal choices by the audience as expressions of *identity*—that can be captured to become a greater source of *value* than the art itself, a distinction that is especially obvious in the popular cultural productions distributed online and through streaming media. It is via this process of choice that *potential values* are realized as *exchange value*, drawing attention to *who* chooses—thus reanimating all the historical biases (racism, sexism, homophobia, et al.) that are colonial responses to "social identity threats." The ideological concern evident in this response to social change mirrors the nineteenth century impacts of photography on painting, but does not exceed them. There is no breaking of art's spell through mass reproduction.[92] Instead the status of art is augmented and expanded, since the social function of art as a proxy for class depends not on the actual inaccessibility of works, but on their perception by the human audience *as* inaccessible, rarified works that are not generally available as commodity products. However, *exclusivity* does not require scarcity, even if it implies it.

The limited quantity of art by any artist creates its rarified status as an empirical fact that both supports and contradicts its use as a token for status display. The capacity to produce more art is tempered by its social function, which machine learning challenges by rendering the proposition of aesthetic simulation described by Jorge Luis Borges' story "Pierre Menard, Author of *Don Quixote*"[93] immanent via the instrumental logic of the database. The generative production of new and original images by AI, such as *The Next Rembrandt* (2016), a 'self-portrait' of the Dutch painter Rembrandt van Rijn[94] [Figure 6], instrumentalizes the attenuation of the artist's reflective judgment implicit in questions of *resemblance*, placing this new work in the same avant-garde lineage as *Fountain* and *CloudPainter*. The machine learning system employed by Bart Korsten and his team at the J. Walter Thompson Amsterdam agency derived this new "Rembrandt" from an existing 'rhizome' defined in/by the database of 346 known paintings that were made by Rembrandt himself.[95] Henceforth, Rembrandt has become data.[96]

Machine learning enables 'technical judgment' to create an instrumentality that replicates the appearance of aesthetic approaches and methods used by the Dutch master. This expression of the ideology of creativity converges on philosopher Martin Heidegger's comments in his essay, "The Question Concerning Technology":

> The Idea "house" displays what anything that is fashioned as a house. Particular, real, and possible houses, in contrast, are changing and transitory derivatives of the *Idea* and this belong to what does not endure. But it can never in any

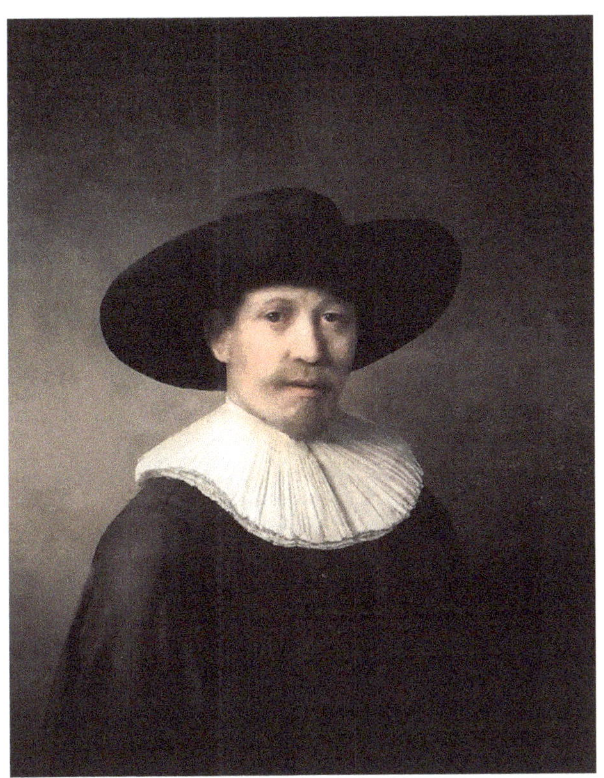

Figure 6: *The Next Rembrandt* (2016) produced by Bart Korsten, art director at the J. Walter Thompson Amsterdam ad agency. This "data visualization" was generated by AI using facial recognition applied to paintings by Rembrandt van Rijn as part of the dataset subjected to machine learning employed to create this image.

> way be established that enduring is based solely on what Plato thinks as *idea* and Aristotle thinks as *τὸ τί ἦν εἶναι* (that which any particular thing has always been) or what metaphysics in its most varied interpretations thinks as *essentia*.[97]

Digital technology converges on philosophy, which provides a precedent for its instrumentalization. These reiterations of Modernist ideology resurface throughout aesthetic automation: the process of recognizing the 'essence of a thing' describes the literal protocol employed by AI—machine learning generates a conceptual model (what Heidegger describes as *Idea*) that allows the emergence of novel works by transforming its idealization into the material presentation that is the art. However, this system is insignificantly "creative"[98] because machine learning does not exceed, can never exceed, the parameters of its sources. What historically appeared to be metaphysical is in fact both materially present and empirical. Despite that powerful limitation, this productive technique makes human agency moot because this synthetic Rembrandt problematizes the aesthetic spectrum shown by Figure 5 that places *novel production* (new) at one end and situates the *restoration* and *recreation* (derivative) employed by "Operation Night Watch" in 2019–2021 to reproduce the entirely missing sections edited out of Rembrandt's painting *The Night Watch* (1642)[99] at the other. Both *The Next Rembrandt* and "Operation Night Watch" create a "painting" that is not 2D computer graphics, but instead employs a 3D printed impasto to reproduce all the features common to Rembrandt's painting (including his use of chiaroscuro, brush strokes, composition, subject matter) were automated to create imagery: balancing unfamiliar and familiar recognitions makes *resemblance* comprehensible.

However, unlike "Operation Night Watch," *The Next Rembrandt* is more than merely a 'style transfer,' or reproduction, or fusion of existing works, but something original, yet without being new—it is literally and technically *derivative*; Korsten's painting-by-AI reveals the social function of *identity* which separates the derivative *resemblance* made by AI from the other *resemblance* of the artist's own *originality*. Artworks with a subservient relationship to another artist (an issue of *identity* used to define *prima causa*) are identified as *derivative* not because the art itself lacks originality, but since its formative organization does. Within this framework, the generative protocol of a machine learning to *be* 'Rembrandt van Rijn' can only produce a *resemblance* that leads to *The Next Rembrandt's* identification as *derivative*—yet all those things that allow the identification of this work as a "Rembrandt self portrait" also demonstrate that what formerly appeared to be *reflective* aesthetic features such as the artist's gesture, signature style, or even personal expression are precisely conventional determinative judgments. They become the degrees of freedom granted to the system by human agency choosing the images that train the models. This process transforms the creative work of reflective judgment into an application of determinative facture that entirely eliminates the future need for the artist in the facture of their own work, disrupting the Enlightenment ideologies of 'originality,' 'genius,' and 'aesthetic value.'[100]

Choice becomes the only factor of aesthetic importance, reiterating Norton's claims for the aesthetic status of Duchamp's *Fountain*. Its ascendancy demonstrates that both reflective (creative) and determinative tasks belong to a spectrum where they overlap and comingle: the automation made possible by machine learning suggests that there might even be rules to 'creativity,' a proposal undermining both the exceptionalism granted to art as an expression of reflective agency (intent) and the ideology that art is a specialized, *human* activity; the rejection of non-human agency in the production of art is a response to this "social identity threat." Machine learning instrumentalizes existing works, abstracting their essential features, which is the purpose of "training" AI systems. These attempts to convert the world into a productive instrumentality reify cultural distinctions between material commodities as *potential values* whose the on-demand production made possible by automation eliminates the need for physical commodity production except in response to specific, individual human desires—all facture becomes bespoke, a radical expansion of the *exclusivity* formerly reserved only for elite audiences.

These aspects of art and intention converge on the expansion of *luxury,* since they question the *utility* of art as a social status token by undermining its *exclusivity*, if not uniqueness. Nevertheless, the *luxury* identified with art is not challenged by changes in technology; the social functions of art always link it to questions of scarcity and rarity via *luxury* that are assumed by its audience. These coincidental parities (art/luxury) render theorizing aesthetics and the social function of art via *luxury* apparently redundant and superfluous. It is precisely the ways that only a few can have a specific production—limited by cost or limited by facture—that defines *luxury* as coterminous with the *exclusivity* of art; thus as an aesthetic category it has lacked the individuation needed to make it comprehensible, because if all /art/ is *luxury*, then the designation and role of *luxury* is identical to that of /art/. AI's aesthetic challenge to /art/ is avoided by the social function of *identity* and the refusal to address *The Next Rembrandt* as an art object,[101] but not resolved. It risks mirroring the nineteenth century rejection of photography–as–art.[102] The historical lineage of refusals of aesthetic status to productions made by a photographic camera (or an AI system) belong to the same cultural trajectory that uses the refusal of industrial production to elevate the status of human handicraft while denigrating machine-based facture; these aesthetics (promoted by William Morris and his Arts and Crafts movement) are a Luddistic rejection of industrialization.[103]

Understanding cultural knowledge as a determinative system governed by *a priori* outcomes returns art to the question of agency apparent in the first "computer art" exhibit of work by computer scientists Bela Julesz and A. Michael Noll at the Howard Wise Gallery in 1965 (and the later MoMA exhibition *The Machine* in 1968). These generative works anticipate contemporary digital systems that automate more complex and dynamic aspects of image creation in both degree and capacity than was possible in 1965.[104] *New York Times* art critic Stuart Preston ended his review with commentary on these future impacts of the computer on artistic intention:

> No matter what the future holds—and scientists predict a time when almost any kind of painting can be computer-generated—the actual touch of the artists will no longer play any part in the making of a work of art. [...] From then on all will be entrusted to the *deus ex machina*. Freed from the tedium of techniques and the mechanics of picture-making, the artist will simply "create."[105]

The "computer art" programmed an *IBM 7094* computer and output as line drawings using a *General Dynamics SC-4020 Microfilm Plotter* that Preston saw attenuates and elides the 'hand of the artist,' continuing the process of eliminating the "tedium of techniques and the mechanics of picture-making" from art that began with photography and which traditional aesthetic evaluations oppose. It is a democratizing process that makes "skilled" facture accessible to all—a *determinative* aesthetic. Preston's specifically negative assessment of "computer art," and by extension the automation possible with AI, transmutes the apperception of art into an aesthetic analogue to the Luddite fallacy when confronting the automated and generative processes of digital production. Accepting digital renderings as objects for aesthetic consideration undermines the established ideology of art that affirms Modernist (Enlightenment) aesthetics as an expression of human agency (intention).

Preston's commentary establishes this heritage as an explicit part of how the computer exceeds the industrial conversion and abstraction of human agency and physical processes into a series of discrete stages *for* production in the assembly line. The steady development of mechanical systems—the typewriter, the video screen, the computer—inform the facture of art while reducing the role of human action in that facture.[106] AI is literally a machine that instrumentalizes reflective judgment by automating aesthetics, thus raising the question of *luxury* directly in how distinctions between conception and implementation parallel the separation of the *mind* (managerial, reflective) from *body* (productive, determinative): the importance of denigrating industrial production maintains aesthetic frameworks that posit an opposition between artists and machinery as a marker of distinction within the societal hierarchy.

Any change to art's social significance poses an ideological challenge to the status quo. A retreat into the antique, unique, and hand made as signs of elite status—tendencies already evident in expansion of *luxury* during the twentieth century—does not necessarily identify a rejection of this cultural heritage so much as an attempt to maintain social status through *exclusivity* despite a democratic broadening of access to bespoke facture; restrictions on this expansion are the foundational appeal of NFTs (non-fungible tokens) where a single owner claims unique "ownership" over a digital work. It is a counter tendency to the 'society of leisure' whose *utility* is crucial, but limited, precisely because scarcity is ultimately incompatible with the expansive demands of capitalist valorization and commodification.

Consciousness of art's social functions unmasks how *art–as–luxury* is an expression of the continuing heritage of racism, sexism and all the biases of class privilege within 'the social.' By radically expanding its address to include its role as a mediator of surveillance and valorization, it simultaneously realizes the nineteenth century demand for art–into–life as a perverse capitalist expansion into 'the social.' However, digital capitalism has transformed the historical conception of *luxury* via behavioral marketing, establishing this narcissistic imaginary as a "price point" in the production of commodities. Although acquiring *luxury* is a demonstration of social status, and *luxury* must circulate to be effective as a token of class distinction,[107] its expansion alters its significance, as the *Culture Track* study shows: transforming art and culture to be more inclusive destroys the museum as necessarily a rarified signifier of social status and position in a reiteration of the problem *resemblance* poses for Kant's philosophy.

By claiming an inherently critical status for art, Modernist philosopher Theodor Adorno attempts to create a distinction within /art/ that would not be subject to these transformations imposed by the dominance of art-as-luxury. While it may appear to reject the capricious subjectivity of capitalist valorization, his argument's concerns with a "Modernist ontology" and an ontological purity for his "critical" art object reflects the same colonial heritage that creates capitalism. He advances an essentialist proposal that denies /art/ is an instrumentalization of ideology through an analysis that affirms its social functions as metaphysical, rather than acknowledging aesthetics' anthropological functions as a proxy for social status and position:

> Their social essence requires a double reflection on [artworks] being-for-themselves and on their relations to society. Their double character is manifest at every point; they change and contradict themselves. [...] Marx's scorn of the pittance Milton received for *Paradise Lost,* a work that did not appear to the market as socially useful labor, is, as a denunciation of useful labor, the strongest defense of art against bourgeois functionalization, which is perpetuated in art's undialectical social condemnation. A liberated society would be beyond the irrationality of its *faux frais* and beyond the ends-means-rationality of *utility*. This is enciphered in art and is the source of art's social explosiveness.[108]

Adorno invokes the inability of art's *exchange value* to predict the prestige of its *use value,* (a contradiction his Marxist analysis cannot accommodate), to argue for a fallacy—that art has a special status that places it *outside* capitalism. His proposition in *Aesthetic Theory* replicates the claim that art must be "functionless" (a special status as an activity independent of *utility* and *use value*). These are the same formalist demands that Greenberg employs in "Modernist Painting" that claimed an essential nature for art that pushes it away from its social functions and the class distinctions it represents. Proposing that "artworks are the plenipotentiaries of things that are no longer distorted by exchange, profit, and the false needs of a degraded humanity"[109] presupposes a lost 'purity' which /art/ then recovers via its waste of labor and resources (*luxury*); it obfuscates any significance of the work in advance, as well as reveals its ideological foundations as a colonial expression of social status and position whose unity and singularity are guaranteed only if its "ontology " remains masked and unquestioned.

Historical aesthetic theories consistently employ metaphysics in an attempt to separate art from decoration (*luxury*), a distinction that allows it to pose as a cultural meditation upon the conditions of reality; this rhetorical exceptionalism is necessary for Adorno's transcendent category of "critical art":

> If thought is in any way to gain a relation to art it must be on the basis that something in reality, something back of the veil spun by the interplay of institutions and false needs, objectively demands art, and it demands an art that speaks for what the veil hides.[110]

His metaphysical arguments are shaped by his personal opposition to the explicitly propagandistic uses for aesthetic production by fascist, authoritarian regimes, but in refusing to address the *use value* and social functions of aesthetics, his analysis replaces one set of ideological claims with a fallacy: the challenge art poses arises directly in its role as a social token for status and position, *not* in a denial of social functions; his "critical art" reaffirms what it attempts to evaluate or challenge in a perverse reversal typical of the ambivalence of social and aesthetic ideologies.

Acknowledging automation is a chimera should not be a surprise when it confronts art: all machines reify the assumptions of their builders. While Adorno assumes that reflective agency creates art in an eerie reiteration of the differential between managerial versus manual agency, his proposal replicates the divisions of both Ruskin and Kant that demarcate between the creative labor of human agency and its mechanical implementation. This convergence on industrial automation anticipates the use of AI to produce art: the role of the artist is to design the mechanism, not to control or manage its operations.

However, technical functions, much like concern with economic relationships, obscures the social dimensions of all AI systems: they always and only operate in response to and addressing human desires. LeWitt's proposal *"The idea becomes a machine that makes the art."*[111] parallels the developments of computer art and the birth of digital automation, mirroring the class separation between managerial decisions (reflective judgment) and their application (determinative labor).This radically reduced aesthetic role—the artist becomes a metaphoric "farmer" who chooses among the productions made by AI systems—is a change in artistic practice to emphasize their agency without concern for facture: this transformation in role corresponds to the proposal made by Duchamp with *Fountain*. It expands the role of "artist" to anyone who interacts with these generative systems—even if that engagement is passive—simply to choose one work in place of another; the potential use of pervasive monitoring in relation to generative art presentations is obvious, an application of surveillance that makes everyone an "artist."

The sovereign disdain for human relationships in digital capitalism reflects demands for increased profits and the drive to seek ever-greater productive efficiency through automation and AI.[112] These recapitulations and reduplications of capitalism and industrial ideology are endemic to art and aesthetics, but become obvious when confronting the economic impacts of this cultural expansion of *luxury* via automation that creates the potential to address the fiscal lacuna between aesthetic works and other types of industrial production that economists William Baumol and William Bowen noted in their study of the performing arts.[113] "Baumol's cost disease" identifies the problem they described: the costs for creative productions has remained *almost* entirely (and resolutely) impervious to the increases in speed and efficiencies made possible by industrial facture and the improvements of automation, yet the wages for creative human labor have steadily increased. AI suggests an avenue that could resolve some of these discrepancies since bespoke on-demand media rendered for singular viewers[114] is nascent in the customized "feeds" of social media or those music streaming services that produce "original" compositions corresponding to the past interests of their listeners.

AI even potentially reduces (or eliminates) some of the spiraling costs Baumol identifies for live performances. A two hour production cannot be transformed into a 1 hour production without fundamental changes to the work, but other aspects of the live production are capable of being automated: initial writing of the script, as well as preproduction design, fabrication, and rehearsal. Finally elements of the performance itself, such as the use of digital actors and generative music. What the audience encounters in AI generated art may not be subject to increases in efficiency, nevertheless, the potential to reduce teh need for creative labor is not the fantasy of automation, but an immanent aspect of how AI is being developed and is implied by its current applications.

Art and capitalism alike express historical ideologies about human agency (intention) that AI exposes as a narcissistic imaginary whose unmasking happens with computer scientist Aidan Meller's Ai-Da painting robot that was included in the *2022 Venice Biennale.* Its 'technical agency' violates that ideology of art which conceives it as a transcendent expression of unique human agency. This rupture with skilled human craftsmanship poses a "social identity threat" that Meller calls an "ethical question."[115]

Once the aesthetic commodity becomes a matching of desire to its fulfillment, (as with the generative productions of AI coupled with their algorithmic distribution), the centrality of *nostalgia* to this continuously updated procession of "new" commodities is revealed as a totalizing abstraction of surveillance that will not provide an alternative to, nor expansion from, its reverie of the already-known precisely because this system only offers *resemblances* that are catalogued and recorded to optimize the match of production to audience in degree and complexity of output. The problem this development poses for art—and the "social identity threat" it creates—results from this generative presentation being indistinguishable from traditional art works made by humans, as aesthetic philosopher Scott Contreras-Koterbay notes:

> It could be claimed that the digital, digital materiality, computationality, autonomous algorithmic entities and/or independent digital agencies are fanciful at best, the subject of science fiction, and impossible as genuinely creative and imaginative artists. These claims, however, almost don't matter. We exist in the digital and, as such, we are unable to see outside of it or without it. As this becomes more and more the case, the question of actual AIs will matter less and less—even if they exist, we won't be able to tell the difference—and their

aesthetic output will become indistinguishable from those of any other human artist.[116]

The human acceptance of these generative artworks stands in opposition to traditional aesthetic concerns with originality, authenticity, and connoisseurship. The capacities of AI to generate *resemblance* ("looks like art") suggests a fundamental reorganization of historical relationships that brings /art/ under the same regime of cost efficiencies and mass production, as other types of commodity facture—the mechanism employed, and the qualia of facture determine the aesthetics of the work, rather than the skill of the artist. AI offers a potential corrective to Baumol's "cost disease" by reducing the need for human labor, if not eliminating it entirely. The Arts and Crafts dictum "by hammer and by hand do all things stand" becomes as irrelevant to these emergent aesthetics as the Modernist concern with ontology. Although Contreras-Koterbay might seem to suggest that machine learning changes nothing significant about art, as this new system of AI generated art emerges, it makes the Romantic and Modernist the ideology of creativity that understands artworks as "functionless," and reserves aesthetic production as a human privilege no longer tenable.[117]

Although this application sounds distinctly dystopian, even antihumanist, the tools for its implementation are already in existence in primitive form, and by reducing 'artistic intention' in aesthetic facture, they emphasize the discernment of the audience. In the case of "writing," for example, the change from handwriting to the typewriter and then the digital computer has greatly facilitated the composition process and rendered the publisher's tasks, from typesetting to "printing," significantly less costly—yet the actual production of the material to be published has already been automated for some texts—and the human readers did not even notice.

Fears the digital computer will displace familiar aesthetics and artistic processes, deprecating their cultural significance and social functions as proxies for class, creates the debates over machinery-in-art.[118] The ideology of creativity has only a limited set of responses to these attenuations of the artist's role in facture, understanding them as a "social identity threat." AI thus returns human agency in art to critical attention via the democratic potential of autonomous bespoke production and its challenge to the *exclusivity* and *luxury* required by social status displays. This expansion transforms historically rarified production (hence, *luxury*) into mundane commodities in an implicit extension of the 'society of leisure.' Eliminating those tokens indicate elite social status and position undermines separations between social classes. Cost, design, rarified materials, and bespoke manufacturing served as proxies expressing social distinctions precisely because they required the skilled human craftsmanship that AI supplants. These changes explicitly render art and aesthetics political expressions of the continuing importance of colonialism and industrialization. Nevertheless, the changes to art, culture, and aesthetics suggested by the emergence of AI do not mean an end to art, any more than an elimination of artists, but rather a transformation of the artist's role in relation to the art object itself; however, the social function of aesthetics is unlikely to change.

The aesthetic and social ramifications of AI are neither utopian nor dystopian; AI is merely a catalyst that reveals the inherited constraints of past ideologies. If, as architect Cedric Price observed, *"Technology is the answer."* then the question to ask is not *"What was the question?"* but simply and directly, *'Who defines the terms of the problem?'* which brings the colonial heritage of industrialism into the analysis.

Attempts to apprehend this technology's direct impacts on 'the social' are muted by their diffusion into the lineage of industrialization that is omnipresent in digital capitalism: the contemporary globalized period is dominated by technologies of surveillance, persuasion, distribution, and attempts to restore the power relationships between the historical imperial centers and their periphery. Geopolitical conflicts reflect the lack of a clear separation of digital capitalism from earlier forms of colonialism. The instability of attempts to reassert or retain this historical dominance, either economically, or by force of arms, leads to fragmentation, volatility, and uncertainty.[119]

By theorizing 'the social' and AI through the societal hierarchy and the "social identity threat" posed to social status and position by changes to established rights, restrictions, and opportunities, the lineage of *identity* unmasks the repressive nature of the semiotic processes of digital capitalism utilizing AI to replace human labor; the trajectory of machinery and industrial mechanisms that amplify the productive capacity of human agency unites threats to social status, applications of this technology, and *who* is being replaced by it. How digital capitalism has already colonized 'the social' through the valorization of *identity* anticipates the future role of AI: this technology is the perfect example of a crystalline system of fixed relationships being used to block development of the 'society of leisure.' Individual and group responses to AI's "social identity threat" that define an interlocking system of bias and dominance makes its impacts on 'the social' more difficult to directly address or identify; the expansion of culture beyond its traditional sites precisely demonstrates these processes in action—they are structural, systemic, and masked—disrupting historical limits to valorization through stable group membership. As these foundations have become subject to flux, variability, and instability, they in turn disrupt the human capacity for rational analysis—which agnotology amplifies.

Paralleling economic functions within 'the social,' AI's cultural impacts arise from attempts to reify ideology as technology, rather than from an internal and innate significance. By replacing reflective judgment with subjective, traditional, and/or irrational beliefs that act to maintain the status quo social hierarchy, change and innovation become disruptive threats, and social status becomes a fixed product of established rules and conventions awaiting valorization. This structure provides order, making the privilege of *leisure* apparent in how its universal expansion to the working classes under industrial capitalism in the nineteenth century was a contentious issue, ultimately enforced through unionization and increased wages; the conception of "wages as lost profits" derives from the effects of this unionization.

AI reminds us that inhumanity is contagious because the status "human" has historically been a class privilege. Limiting human agency to the confines established by an autonomous process supplants the intelligence of skilled crafts people with rote unintelligence, rendering human agency as the merely linkages between mechanical operations on an assembly line, a prophylactic disenfranchisement that exacerbates industrialism's role in maintaining social status and position. The expansion of this compartmentalization associates human labor with the machine, justifying the social position of human labor as socially inferior because their thought and agency are restricted—evoking Descartes's dictum "*cogito ergo sum,*" and the mirroring the literal meaning of *homo sapiens* as the *thinking man*—to enable a classist, sexist, and racist reservation of the status "human" for only white, elite (cis-male) groups. This cultural baggage informs contemporary concerns with *identity* as the signifier of 'human' that is the heritage of civil rights and anti-colonial movements: the demand for the same status and rights accorded to 'humans' (the dominant elite classes). The extension of status brings the role of "social identity threats" within digital capitalism to the fore, (much like the interlocking supports of *identity, luxury,* and *leisure*), and activates agnotology as a mechanism of social control in response to these challenges: the tendency of digital capitalism to isolate and magnify existing biases is not simply an issue of machine learning, but of its interaction with the existing *de facto* inequalities and injustices of society itself.

Thus, culture is possibly the most dramatic technology that AI automates. 'Technical agency' suggests that what appeared to be metaphysical and noumenal can be radically isolated as empirical features of the world, transforming what began as ideological or political decisions into instrumental technologies whose change or replacement becomes unimaginable; the social functions and acknowledgments of art and aesthetics are transformations and challenges to that *use value* revealed by redefining capitalism as a *system expressing social class* through commodity production and use, i.e. a system that manages access and distribution, rather than as *the commodification of agency*. Thus by automating aspects of aesthetic appraisal, the AI system transforms them into apparati, a series of modular decisions, interlocking as the same mundane operations of digital technology in general.

Digital capitalism, despite its protean capacity for the expansion of commercial markets and its capacities to transform social relationships into new values, lacks resilience to the vicissitudes of life it creates. Blocking discourse via agnotology is necessary for its valorization of semiotic production to occur: rendering the terms of discussion ambiguous and ambivalent establishes all alternatives as valid and immanent, facilitating the transformation of *potential value* into *value*. This fragile system requires constant reinforcement and protection against new challenges and social opposition even though it has an unparalleled capacity for political capture at the levels of jurisprudence and (inter)national policy.

The instabilities that emerged with the start of the Covid-19 pandemic in 2020 are not fiscal or logistical failures, but demonstrations of how just-in-time delivery and production has almost no capacity to accommodate disruptions to its global supply chains and distribution or social challenges to its dominance: this network of immaterial flows and physical marketplaces does not escape the constraints of materiality, even if digital capitalism specifically imagines that the material limits of the world no longer apply to its machinations. In the shadow of the pandemic, the question posed by this analysis, '*Whose labor is automated by AI?*' turns from the instrumentalities of technology to their expressions in human culture and society as "social identity threats," forcing an acknowledgment that AI and the digital are entangled with *identity*—and therefore complicit with the evolution of colonialism into globalization. Unlike the digital's impacts on labor, economics, or technical systems, the convergence of autonomous machines and human culture—unless approached as an exercise in the literary criticism of sci-fi—remains largely hidden. Instrumentalized biases (including racism, sexism, and ageism) are not distortions of the training data used by machine learning, they are inherent features of human society that police the boundaries of "social identity." Although AI instrumentalizing bias is both well known and readily apparent, its socio-cultural impacts remain as difficult to quantify as they are to isolate, since injustice and privation are not exclusive products of automation.

The potential expansion of the 'society of leisure' proffered in the fantasy of automation places traditional capitalist valorization under pressure via the mismatch between limitations in productive capacity versus the constraints of *utility*: *leisure* is both the product of 'labor saving devices' and their antithesis, a result accumulated through the displacement of human action. Unlike *idleness* which is always enforced by an external agency that does not require labor, 'labor saved' leaves *leisure* as its product. The required labor that is now-performed by machine leaves time available for other pursuits. Entire industries have emerged to exploit this available time, an outcome that reifies the transcendence of physicality in/by the aura of the digital, valorizing activities as *leisure* while rendering them regimented and productive—a sleight of hand that uses the threat of *idleness* as a mechanism to prompt consumption; the mass culture that emerged after World War II in the United States specifically exploited this dichotomy to replace the producerist culture of traditional craft promoted by the Arts and Crafts movement reformers in the nineteenth century.

Digital capitalism employs pervasive monitoring to recover the "waste" of *leisure* and all other everyday activities as valorization opportunities; semiotic facture within the database then uses this data to facilitate the transformation of *potential values* into *value*. Linking *leisure* to consumption also connects it to *identity* through the social role of consumption as an expression of "self" that dominates digital capitalism. The historical act of self-definition becomes a self-valorization that conceives of 'the self' as a conglomeration of products consumed, media viewed, and brands owned; the individual becomes coterminous with the data collected about them—but it also endows industrial commodities with the same aura of exclusivity and privilege as any other token for social significance. This intermediation of *identity* through consumption reinforces the role that *leisure* now plays as a specific type of commodity whose function as a proxy for social status and positions necessitates the expansion of address by "arts and culture" beyond its elite origins. This reconception of *leisure* as a consumptive work avoids the socially disruptive potentials an expansion of rights and privileges might otherwise produce. AI is the vehicle for this capture, and the mechanism preserving existing hierarchies and social status in a pathological attempt to eliminate its "social identity threat" by preserving the *status quo*. The question to ask of all autonomous, automated, and technical agencies may begin with *whose agency is automated*, but must ultimately confront those whose position in 'the social' is maintained by that automation.

notes

1 Perelman, M. *The Invention of Capitalism: Classical Political Economy and the Secret History of Primitive Accumulation* (Durham: Duke University Press, 2000).

2 Munn, L. *Automation is a Myth* (Redwood City: Stanford University Press, 2022).

3 Christian, B. *The Alignment Problem: Machine Learning and Human Values* (New York: W.W. Norton and Company, 2020).

4 Benanav, A. *Automation and the Future of Work* (New York: Verso, 2020).

5 Rose, N. "The Death of the Social? Re-Figuring the Territory of Government" *Economy and Society* vol. 25, no. 3 (1996) p. 329.

6 Baudrillard, J. *In the Shadow of the Silent Majorities ... or the End of the Social* (New Haven: Semiotexte(e), 1983).

7 Foucault, M. *The Birth of Biopolitics: Lectures at the Collège de France 1978–1979* (Palgrave Macmillan, 2010) p. 297.

8 Veblen, T. *The Theory of the Leisure Class* (New York: Dover, 1994).

9 Deleuze, G. and Guattari, F. *Anti-Oedipus* trans. Robert Hurley, Mark Seem and Helen R, Lane (Minneapolis: University of Minnesota Press, 1983) pp.224-227.

10 Muro, M.; Maxim, R.; Whiton, J. *Automation and Artificial Intelligence: How Machines are Affecting People and Places* (Washington: Brookings Institute, 2019) p. 5.

11 Muro, M.; Whiton, J.; Maxim, R. *What Jobs are Affected by AI? Better-Paid, Better-Educated Workers Face the Most Exposure* (Washington: Brookings Institute, 2019), p. 11. https://www.brookings.edu/wp-content/uploads/2019/11/2019.11.20_BrookingsMetro_What-jobs-are-affected-by-AI_Report_Muro-Whiton-Maxim.pdf released November 19, 2019.

12 Hye Jin Rho; Brown, H.; Fremstad, S. *A Basic Demographic Profile of Workers in Frontline Industries* (Washington: Center for Economic and Policy Research, 2020).

13 Marazzi, C. *The Violence of Financial Capitalism: New Edition* (Los Angeles: Semiotexte, 2011) pp. 43-64.

14 Debord, G. *The Society of the Spectacle* trans. Donald Nicholson-Smith (New York: Zone Books, 1994).

15 Morgan, R. *The End of the Art World* (New York: Allworth Press, 1998).

16 Burgess, J. "All Your Chocolate Rain Are Belong To US? Viral Video, Youtube and the Dynamics of Participatory Culture" *Video Vortex Reader: Responses to Youtube* ed. Geert Lovink and Sabine Niederer (Amsterdam: Institute of Network Cultures, 2008) pp. 101-110.

17 Polanyi, K. *The Great Transformation* (Boston: Beacon Press, 2001).

18 Archer, J. *Social Unrest and Popular Protest in England, 1780–1840* (New York: Cambridge University Press, 2000) pp. 42-56.

19 Benanav, A. *Automation and The Future of Work* (New York: Verso, 2020) pp. 15-28.

20 Čapek's play *Rossumovi Univerzální Roboti (Rossum's Universal Robots)*, first produced in 1921, is the story of a robot rebellion.

21 Federici, S. *Caliban and the Witch* (Brooklyn: Autonomedia, 2004) pp. 21-60.

22 The 19th Ammendmentment to the *United States Constitution*, ratified August 18, 1920.

23 Ruskin, J. *The Stones of Venice, vol. II* (Project Gutenberg eBook, 2009) p. 161.

24 Pevsner, N. *Pioneers of Modern Design* (Bath: Palazzo Editions, 2011) pp. 36-57.

25 Betancourt, M. *Research Art: glitches, poetics, typography and the aura of the digital* (Savannah: I'm Press'd, 2021) pp. 41-54.

26 Dann, K. *Bright Colors, Falsely Seen* (New Haven: Yale, 1998).

27 Kaplan, W. "The Art That Is Life" *The Arts and Crafts Movement in America, 1875–1920.* (Boston: Museum of Fine Arts, 1987).

28 Benjamin, W. "The Work of Art in the Age of Mechanical Reproduction," *Illuminations*, trans. Harry Zohn, (New York: Schocken Books, 1969).

29 Kleemann, B. "I Put This Moment Here" *Wunderkammer* ed. Birgit Kleemann (Berlin: Brooklyn Fine Arts and Autocenter-Verlag

30 Johnson, W. *The Broken Heart of America: St. Louis and the Violent History of the United States* (New York: Basic Books, 2020) pp. 181-216.

31 Marx, K. *The Grundrisse (The Fragment on Machines)* (London: Penguin Classics Reprint edition: 1993) p. 692.

32 Ford, M. *The Lights in the Tunnel: Automation, Accelerating Technology and the Economy of the Future* (New York: Acculant Publishing, 2009).

33 Dann, K. *Bright Colors Falsely Seen,* (New Haven: Yale, 1998) pp. 94-95.

34 Lears, T. *No Place of Grace: Anti-Modernism and the Transformation of American Culture, 1880-1920*, (New York: Pantheon, 1981) pp. 19-22.

35 There is extensive research on this proposition; see for example, J.-T. Lee and C.-S. Kim, "Image aesthetic assessment based on pairwise comparison a unified approach to score regression, binary classification, and personalization" *Proceedings of the IEEE/CVF International Conference on Computer Vision* (*ICCV*) (October 2019).

36 Betancourt, M. *The Critique of Digital Capitalism* (Brooklyn: Punctum Books, 2016) pp. 191-214.

37 McIlroy-Young, R; Wang, R.; Sen, S.; Kleinberg, J.; Anderson, A. "Detecting Individual Decision-Making Style: Exploring Behavioral Stylometry in Chess" *35th Conference on Neural Information Processing Systems (NeurIPS 2021)*, Sydney, Australia 2021.

38 Jemio, D.; Hagerty, A.; Aranda, F. "The Case of the Creepy Algorithm That 'Predicted' Teen Pregnancy" *Wired* (February 16, 2022) https://www.wired.com/story/argentina-algorithms-pregnancy-prediction/

39 Saul, J. and Baptista, E. "Off the grid: Chinese data law adds to global shipping disruption" *Reuters* (November 17, 2021) retrieved December 20, 2021 https://www.reuters.com/world/china/off-grid-chinese-data-law-adds-global-shipping-disruption-2021-11-17/

40 LaPlaca Cohen. *Culture Track '17* (New York: Culture Track, 2017) pp. 6-7. https://s28475.pcdn.co/wp-content/uploads/2019/06/CT2017-Top-Line-Report.pdf

41 Bourriaud, N. *Relational Aesthetics* (Dijon-Quetigny: les presses du réel, 2004).

42 Cahill, H. "Art for the Millions," *Art Digest* 7:5 (December 1, 1932) p. 4.

43 Mould, O. *Against Creativity* (New York: verso, 2018) pp.83-94.

44 MacDougall, I. and Simpson, I. "A libertarian 'startup city' in Honduras faces its biggest hurdle: the locals" *Rest of the World* (October 5, 2021) https://restofworld.org/2021/honduran-islanders-push-back-libertarian-startup/

45 Taylor, F. *The Principles of Scientific Management* (New York: Harper, 1911) p. 39.

46 Simondon, G. *On the Mode of Existence of Technical Objects* (Minneapolis: University of Minnesota Press, 2017).

47 Mould, O. *Against Creativity* (New York: verso, 2018) pp. 17-53.

48 Critical Art Ensemble. *The Electronic Disturbance* (Brooklyn: Autonomedia, 1994).

49 Frey, C.B.; Osborne, M.A. "The Future of Employment: How Susceptible are Jobs to Computerization?" *Technological Forecasting and Social Change,* vol. 114 (January 2017) pp. 254-280.

50 Betancourt, M. *Force Magnifier: the cultural impacts of artificial intelligence* (Cabin John: Wildside Press, 2020) p. 130.

51 Steryl, H. "Culture and Crime" *e-flux*, May 16, 2022. https://www.e-flux.com/notes/468843/culture-and-crime

52 Marx, K. *Capital: Volume 1* (London: Penguin Classics Reprint edition: 1990) pp. 8-9.

53 Kant, I. "IV. On Judgment as a Power that Legislates A Priori" *The Critique of Judgment,* trans. Werner Pluhar (Indianapolis: Hackett Publishing Company, 1987) 179-181.

54 Acemoglu, D. and Restrepo, P. "Automation and New Tasks. How Technology Displaces and Reinstates Labor" *Journal of Economic Perspectives* vol. 33, no. 2 (Spring 2019) pp. 3-30.

55 Kant, I. "Section 1: Pure Reason in its Dogmatic Use" *The Critique of Pure Reason,* trans. Werner Pluhar (Indianapolis: Hackett Publishing Company, 1996) p. 675.

56 Graeber, D. *Debt: The First 5,000 Years* (Brooklyn: Melville House, 2014) pp. 165-168.

57 Greenberg, C. "Modernist Painting" *The Collected Essays and Criticism: Vol. 4* (Chicago: University of Chicago Press, 1955) p. 85.

58 Betancourt, M. “Visual Music and Abstraction: From Avant-Garde Synaesthesia to Digital Technesthesia” *Iconology of Abstraction: Non-Figurative Images and the Modern World (Advances in Art and Visual Studies)*, ed. Krešimir Purgar (Routledge, 2020) pp. 143-159.

59 Dann, K. *Bright Colors Falsely Seen,* (New Haven: Yale, 1998) pp. 91; 94-95.

60 Betancourt, M. “Chance Operations / Limiting Frameworks: Sensitive Dependence on Initial Conditions” in *Tout-Fait* Vol. 2, No. 4, 2002.

61 Breton, A. *Manifestoes of Surrealism* trans. Richard Seaver and Helen R. Lane (Ann Arbor: University of Michigan Press, 1972).

62 Betancourt, M. *Research Art: glitches, poetics, typography and the aura of the digital* (Savannah: I'm Press'd, 2021) pp. 41-54.

63 Loos, A “Ornament and Crime” *Crime and Ornament: The Arts and Popular Culture in the Shadow of Adolf Loos* ed. Bernie Miller and Melony Ward, (New York: XYZ Books, 2002) pp. 29-30.

64 Taylor, H. *Art and the Intellect: Moral Values and the Experience of Art* (New York: The Museum of Modern Art, 1960) pp. 41-62.

65 Muro, M.; Whiton, J.; Maxim, R. *What Jobs are Affected by AI? Better-Paid, Better-Educated Workers Face the Most Exposure* (Washington: Brookings Institute, 2019), p. 11. https://www.brookings.edu/wp-content/uploads/2019/11/2019.11.20_BrookingsMetro_What-jobs-are-affected-by-AI_Report_Muro-Whiton-Maxim.pdf released November 19, 2019.

66 Marx, K. *Capital: Volume 1* (London: Penguin Classics Reprint edition: 1990) p. 9.

67 Wolkenstein, C. *The Horn of Plenty: A Brief Theory of Luxury* (Düsseldorf: Optik Books, 2021).

68 Werner, P. *Museum, Inc.: Inside the Global Art World* (Chicago: Prickly Paradigm Press, 2005).

69 Eco, U. "Interpreting Serials" *The Limits of Interpretation* (Bloomington: University of Indiana Press, 1994).

70 Betancourt, M. *The Digital Agent versus Human Agency* (Cabin John: Wildside Press, 2020).

71 Betancourt, M. "The 'intentional function' in still and moving photographic images" *Semiotica*, vol 2022, no 246, 2022.

72 Norton, L. "The Richard Mutt Case" *The Blind Man* no. 2 (1917) p. 5.

73 Hebdige,D. *Subculture: The Meaning of Style* (New York: Methuen, 1979).

74 Florida, R. "Bohemia and Economic Geography" *Journal of Economic Geography* no. 2 pp. 55–71 (2002).

75 Baudrillard, J. *Passwords* (New York: Verso, 2003)

76 Morgan, R. *The End of the Art World* (New York: Allworth Press, 1998).

77 Rothkoff, S. *Roxy Paine* (New York: James Cohan Gallery, 2001) pp. 21-25.

78 Greenberg, C. "Modernist Painting" *The Collected Essays and Criticism: Vol. 4* (Chicago: University of Chicago Press, 1955) p. 85.

79 Zylinska, J. *AI Art: Machine Visions and Warped* Dreams (London: Open Humanities Press, 2020).

80 Foster, H. *Design and Crime (and Other Diatribes)* (New York: Verso, 2002) pp. 43-62.

81 Danto, A. *The Transfiguration of the Commonplace* (Cambridge: Harvard University Press, 1981) pp. 115-135.

82 Robinson, H. "Paradoxes of Art, Science and Photography (1892)" *Photographers on Photography: Foundations of Modern Photography Series* ed. Nathan Lyons (Englewood Cliffs: Pren-tice-Hall, 1966) p. 86.

83 Danto, A. *The Transfiguration of the Commonplace* (Cambridge: Harvard University Press, 1981) pp. 94-95.

84 MacCarthy, F. *Anarchy & Beauty: William Morris and His Legacy 1860–1960* (London: National Portrait Gallery, 2014) pp. 59-75.

85 Krauss, R. *The Originality of the Avant-Garde and Other Myths* (Cambridge: The MIT Press, 1985).

86 Hulten, K. *The Machine as seen as the end of the mechanical age* (New York: Museum of Modern Art, 1968).

87 LeWitt, Sol. "Sentences on Conceptual Art, 1968" *Conceptual Art* ed. Ursula Meyer (New York: Dutton, 1972) pp. 174-175.

88 Rosen, B. *The Corporate Search for Visual Identity* New York: Van Norstrand Reinhold Company, 1970).

89 Contreras-Koterbay, S. "The Teleological Nature of Digital Aesthetics—the New Aesthetic in Advance of Artificial Intelligence" *AM Journal of Art and Media Studies* no. 20 (2019) p. 105. DOI: 10.25038/am.v0i20.326.

90 Wolkenstein, C. *The Horn of Plenty: A Brief Theory of Luxury* (Düsseldorf: Optik Books, 2021) pp. 47-54.

91 Rosinger, K. "What Shall We Look for in Art?" *The Journal of Philosophy*, vol. 34, no. 12 (June 10, 1937) p. 309.

92 Abbing, H. *Why are Artists Poor? The Exceptional Economy of the Arts* (Amsterdam: Amsterdam University Press, 2004) p. 307.

93 Borges, J. "Pierre Menard, Author of *Don Quixote*" *Ficciones*

94 Pickett-Groen, N. "The Next Rembrandt: bringing the Old Master back to life" *Medium*, posted January 24, 2018 https://medium.com/@DutchDigital/the-next-rembrandt-bringing-the-old-master-back-to-life-35dfb1653597

95 Gillick, L. "The Good of Work" *Are You Working Too Much? Post-Fordism, Precarity, and the Labor of Art* ed. Julieta Ardanda, Brian Kuan Wood, and Anton Vidokle (Berlin: Sternberg Press, 2011) pp. 70-72.

96 Shaviro, S. *Post Cinematic Affect* (Washington: Zero Books, 2010), pp. 132-133.

97 Heidegger, M. *The Question Concerning Technology* (New York: Harper Perennial, 1982) pp. 30.

98 Kant, I. "Section 1: Pure Reason in its Dogmatic Use" *The Critique of Pure Reason,* trans. Werner Pluhar (Indianapolis: Hackett Publishing Company, 1996) p. 675.

99 Furtula, A. "Research, restoration begins on Rembrandt's 'Night Watch'" *Associated Press* (July 8, 2019); Davis-Marks, I. "Lost Edges of Rembrandt's 'Night Watch' Are Restored Using Artificial Intelligence" *Smithsonian Magazine* (June 25, 2021).

100 Partch, H. *Genesis of a Music* (Madison: University of Wisconsin Press, 1949).

101 Kazakina, K. "AI-Generated Portrait Sells for $432,500 in an Auction First" *Bloomberg News,* October 25, 2018, 3:22 PM EDT; updated October 25, 2018, 3:41 PM EDT; retrieved October 25, 2018.

102 Robinson, H. "Paradoxes of Art, Science and Photography (1892)" (Englewood Cliffs, Prentice-Hall, 1966) pp. 82-88.

103 Kaplan, W. "The Lamp of British Precedent: An Introduction to the Arts and Crafts Movement" *"The Art That Is Life": The Arts and Crafts Movement in America, 1875-1920* (Boston: Bulfinch, 1987) pp. 52-60.

104 Zylinska, J. *AI Art: Machine Visions and Warped Dreams* (London: Open Humanities Press, 2020).

105 Preston, St. "Reputations Made and in the Making: Art ex Machina" *The New York Times*, Sunday, April 18, 1965 p. 366.

106 Kittler, F. *Gramophone, Film, Typewriter* (Stanford: Stanford University Press, 1999).

107 Wolkenstein, C. *The Horn of Plenty: A Brief Theory of Luxury* (Düsseldorf: Optik Books, 2021).

108 Adorno, T. *Aesthetic Theory* (Minneapolis: University of Minnesota Press, 1998) p. 227.

109 Adorno, T. *Aesthetic Theory* (Minneapolis: University of Minnesota Press, 1998) p. 227.

110 Adorno, T. *Aesthetic Theory* (Minneapolis: University of Minnesota Press, 1998) p. 18.

111 Lippard, L. *Six Years: The Dematerialization of the Art Object* (Berkeley: The University of California Press, 1997) p. 28.

112 Schumpeter, J. *Capitalism, Socialism, and Democracy* (New York: Harper Perennial, 2008) pp. 31-32.

113 Baumol, W. and Bowen, W. *The Performing Arts: The Economic Dilemma* (New York: The Twentieth Century Fund, 1966).

114 Betancourt, M. *Force Magnifier: The Cultural Impacts of Artificial Intelligence* (Cabin John: Wildside Press, 2020) pp. 77-78.

115 Davies, C. "'Mind-blowing': Ai-Da becomes first robot to paint like an artist" *The Guardian* (April 4, 2022) https://www.theguardian.com/technology/2022/apr/04/mind-blowing-ai-da-becomes-first-robot-to-paint-like-an-artist

116 Contreras-Koterbay, S. "The Teleological Nature of Digital Aesthetics—the New Aesthetic in Advance of Artificial Intelligence" *AM Journal of Art and Media Studies* no. 20 (2019) p. 105. DOI: 10.25038/am.v0i20.326.

117 Harris, R. *The Great Debate About Art* (Chicago: Prickly Paradigm Press, 2010).

118 Ngai, S. *Our Aesthetic Categories: Zany, Cute, Interesting* (Cambridge: Harvard University Press, 2102) pp. 197, 227-228.

119 The Invisible Committee. *The Coming Insurrection* (Los Angeles: Semiotexte, 2009).

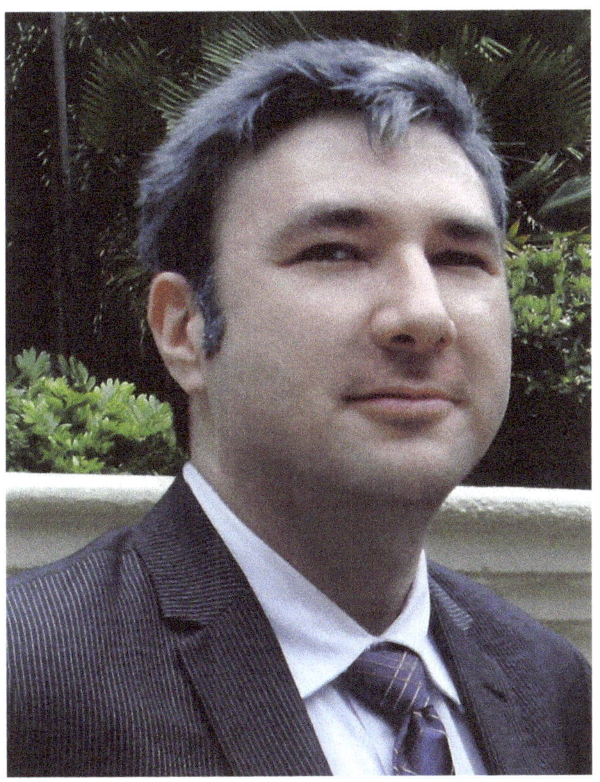

Michael Betancourt is a critical theorist and research artist concerned with digital technology and capitalist ideology. His writing considers the social and cultural impacts of AI, Bitcoin, surveillance, and Universal Basic Income (inter alia) as reflections of structural demands implicit in how the European Enlightenment informs both historical industrial capitalism and contemporary digital technology. His writing has been translated into Chinese, French, German, Greek, Italian, Persian, Portuguese, and Spanish. His online archive is located at *michaelbetancourt.com*

www.ingramcontent.com/pod-product-compliance
Ingram Content Group UK Ltd.
Pitfield, Milton Keynes, MK11 3LW, UK
UKHW062253290726
14090UKWH00017B/663

9 780979 321542